GOVERNMENT AND INDUSTRY SERIES
General Editors: J B Heath and T C Evans

2 PRIVATE ENTERPRISE AND
PUBLIC INTERVENTION

The Courtaulds Experience

PRIVATE ENTERPRISE AND PUBLIC INTERVENTION

The Courtaulds Experience

Arthur Knight

London · George Allen & Unwin Ltd
Ruskin House   Museum Street

ISBN 0 04 338068 9   hardback
     0 04 338069 7   paperback

Printed in Great Britain
in 11 point Times Roman type
by T & A Constable Ltd
Hopetoun Street, Edinburgh

Editors' Note

That successive governments have mismanaged their relations with British industry seems undeniable. What exactly is wrong, and what are the problems in putting it right, are less easily discerned. Many observers are now asking questions of this kind; they are acutely aware of the importance to this country of finding answers.

The series of books we are editing examines how governments manage their relations with industry, what the objectives appear to be, how firms manage their responses, and with what effects. There is also a strong prescriptive element running through it. How should government–industry relations be managed, what improvements seem desirable and feasible?

Arthur Knight is Deputy Chairman of Courtaulds, one of Britain's largest enterprises. The book he has written is a personal record of his own experience as a senior executive, and of the firm in which he has worked for over thirty years, in relation to government. He has put government policies and actions in their context, as part of the environment which shapes business decisions. He has used his experience to highlight the problems raised for firms—his firm in particular—by pursuit in government of 'The Public Interest', which supposedly guides so many of their actions. In so doing he has written a valuable documentary on the last ten years of Courtaulds, with insights into the realities of being a senior executive that will stand as an important and unique contribution to the study of management education.

An earlier volume in the series was published recently. It was written by the Rt Hon Edmund Dell, MP, a former Minister of State at the Board of Trade and at the Department of Employment and Productivity. While the present volume perceives the problems of government–industry relations through the eyes of a senior executive in British industry,

Edmund Dell has written about the same subject through the eyes of a politician, a Minister of the Crown who exercised major responsibilities in relation to British industry. The fact that these two leaders in their own fields had sometimes confronted each other in discussion and negotiation, and in their books sometimes touch on the same topics, adds interest and insight into what each has written.

These first two volumes in the series represent only the personal views of the two authors. Each author was encouraged to explore his understanding of the problem in his own way, and neither had a mandate to review or represent any particular range of topics. We felt also that the authors should express themselves in their own individual ways—we had no wish at all to impose uniformity in style or approach.

Of course the views of the authors do not necessarily represent the generality of senior executives or Ministers of the Crown. Nevertheless, as persons who have risen high in their chosen professions, who have had much relevant experience, and who clearly have thought deeply about these experiences, what they have to say is of considerable general interest in understanding more about—and hopefully improving upon—the management of government–industry relations.

The authors of these volumes each had the opportunity to read the manuscript of the other, but only when his own had reached the 'final draft' stage. Each author has added some comments on what the other has written.

There are other volumes in preparation. While these two in the series adopt a 'top-down' approach, two others will adopt rather more of a 'bottom-up' approach in which the same problems will be seen from a quite different standpoint—that of the analysist, both theoretical and practical. Another volume will analyse the special problems of local government, and of their relations with the central government and with industry. A final volume will survey all these specialist contributions and will draw more general conclusions.

London Graduate   *J B Heath*
School of   *T C Evans*
Business Studies   *December 1972*

Preface

The purpose of this study is threefold: first, to examine the development of Courtaulds, largely from 1962 onwards, the objectives which management were seeking to attain and the methods adopted; secondly, to examine government policies and actions during these years as they impinged upon the company, the apparent purposes which these were intended to serve and the methods adopted; and finally to analyse the interactions between these two. The study is written from the viewpoint of a senior executive who has been closely involved throughout. The writer joined the company as a junior economist in 1939, returned in 1946 after six years in the army to work almost wholly concerned with the company's overseas interests until appointed to the Board in 1958. Then followed a period of nearly three years as one of the diversification team until appointment as finance director in 1961 just before the ICI bid, which appointment was held until 1970.

The value of such a study of a single enterprise and its experiences in the field of government–industry relations is seen to lie in its concern with the problems of a specific situation rather than with the more general issues with which public policies are necessarily concerned, and it should thus provide a test of the effectiveness of those policies. In particular it permits an assessment of the impact on a single enterprise of the variety of objectives which governments have sought to achieve in the public interest, and of the administrative instruments for doing this.

The study falls into two sections. The first serves two purposes. It describes the scene which puts subsequent sections into their historical and environmental context. It also describes how management went about formulating strategy, how major decisions were arrived at and carried out. A large part of the specific relationships between Courtaulds and government arose out of these decisions. The first part is a necessary prelude to understanding the second and third parts.

The second section examines interactions with government in three broad groups—those affecting the textile industry or important parts of it in which Courtaulds played a leading role, those specific to Courtaulds as an individual firm, and those of wider generality affecting all firms and industries, in which Courtaulds was but one of many.

This section also attempts to assess the effects of these interactions on Courtaulds and on the public interest, and to draw some lessons.

My colleagues at Courtaulds gave the project their support and encouragement. In carrying it through I have had much practical help, in particular from Janine Gandon whose many contributions included preparing material for Chapters 5, 6, and 7. The book could not have been written without her. In preparing the earlier chapters Bernardine Gregory's knowledge of the company's records was invaluable. Glenys Webb coped patiently with the typing.

John Heath as editor guided and goaded throughout with great tact and patience. Sir Richard Powell, Sir Richard Clarke and Professor Donald Coleman read the text and made comments which were critical, stimulating and helpful, giving generously of their time. I alone am responsible for the final text.

ARTHUR KNIGHT

December 1972

Contents

PART 2   COURTAULDS AND THE GOVERNMENT

Appendices

Part One

THE GROWTH OF COURTAULDS

Chapter One

THE SEARCH FOR A STRATEGY

The year 1962 was in many ways a watershed for Courtaulds. The ICI attempted takeover was successfully repulsed. The new management team took control. And there was initiated in that period the intensification of Courtaulds' development into a vertical fibre–textile business, shifting its emphasis from the earlier preoccupation with fibre manufacture towards its present structure, which now also embraces the whole range of fibre-using activities. 1962 also marked the beginning of the review of policy on competition which led to the Monopolies and Mergers Act of 1965, an Act which influenced so many of the government actions affecting Courtaulds.

The first chapter is concerned with the years before 1962, which set the corporate framework within which the post-1962 management had to operate. They also provided the individuals who formed the post-1962 management team with the experiences which led to their strong views about the way in which Courtaulds should develop, about the style of management that would be appropriate, and about the textile industry generally. For those individuals, the ten years or so before 1962 were educational and formative. They were in sufficiently senior positions to have a fairly full knowledge of what was going on, and some limited influence, but they did not carry the full responsibility.

The more remote past is less relevant to this study because it had little influence on the individuals who were responsible in the post-1962 period. And it is, of course, well documented in Professor Coleman's two-volume history.[1] A few salient

[1] D C Coleman, *Courtaulds: An Economic and Social History* (Oxford University Press, 1969).

features of the 1950s are helpful in understanding the attitudes which were adopted by the new management team of the 1960s.

THE YEARS TO 1957

Importance of viscose

In this period the company was almost wholly dependent for its profits on its cellulosic (rayon) fibre activities in the UK, and of these viscose fibres were far more important than acetate fibres. (Readers not familiar with these terms should refer to Appendix *A*).

The viscose fibres comprise filament textile yarn which is used directly for the production of knitted and woven fabrics; viscose industrial yarn used primarily as reinforcing material in the manufacture of tyres; and viscose rayon staple which is spun into yarns using the cotton, woollen or linen spinning systems before then being used for the manufacture of knitted or woven fabrics or carpets. In 1957, for example, when the Group earned profits of £15M before tax, the only activities apart from viscose fibres which contributed more than £1M were a dividend of £1.2M from British Nylon Spinners and pre-tax profits of £2.4M from British Cellophane.

The attitude towards expansion prospects at the beginning of this period is indicated in the statement of the Chairman, Mr J Hanbury Williams (later Sir John), to the shareholders in July 1952: 'The peak of our first post-war expansion plans is now well passed, and the rate of investment in new buildings and plant has consequently been reduced.' Indeed, in the early 1950s the only major investment project in the UK was for the manufacture of viscose rayon staple at Grimsby.

Overseas interests

There was, however, a considerable preoccupation with expansion overseas. The construction of a dissolving pulp plant in South Africa was begun in 1952 to provide the basic raw material for rayon staple and for Cellophane; otherwise these overseas activities did not relate closely to the company's main business in the UK. The Australian project, for the manufacture of tyre and of acetate yarns, announced at the end of 1949, represented the culmination of negotiations arising from Australia's wartime difficulties in obtaining fibre supplies and was embarked upon by Courtaulds with considerable hesitation—only too justified in the event.

In Canada the market was not big enough to support a viable viscose fibre industry, but the plant originally started in 1926 was considerably enlarged and modernised. In France a small viscose plant was competing with the large CTA concern, and was thus facing problems similar to those which led to the disappearance in the 1950s of all the smaller producers in the UK. In Germany Courtaulds had only 50 per cent of a single-plant company of which the other 50 per cent was owned by its major German competitor. In Italy Courtaulds' interest consisted in a minority stake in Snia Viscosa with no participation in management. In the USA substantial efforts were made to establish a new base following the wartime loss of the formerly successful Courtaulds-owned American Viscose Corporation, and these led in 1952 to the establishment of a viscose rayon staple plant in Alabama.

Small profits were made from time to time by one or other of these activities but they made no important contribution to the Group's results. However, they received much attention by senior management, in part perhaps a result of the then Chairman's earlier pre-war involvement in the company's overseas activities, and in part a consequence of the memory of that decade in the 1930s when dividends from American Viscose alone provided more than the trading profits earned from all of the Group's other activities.

Internal preoccupations
The other major preoccupation of senior management of these years appears to have been discussing schemes of reorganisation. Both in 1950 and in 1957 such reorganisation schemes clearly absorbed much time and attention. It is almost as if the absence of any clear sense of strategic direction led people to an excessive preoccupation with dividing amongst the various members of the Board the responsibility for administering that which already existed.

However, considerable progress was made in these years in building up a research team under the direction of Mr A H Wilson, FRS (later Sir Alan) who had joined the company in 1946 and became research director soon afterwards. This was to prove important in later years, not only for the developments for which it was responsible but also in providing a pool of talent from which many senior managers in later years were to emerge. The objects of this expansion of the research effort were seen as keeping in the forefront of technological advance in the textile industry, improving the properties of existing types of rayon, and exploring the possibilities of new synthetic fibres.

A large proportion of the research effort was directly related to the post-war expansion of capacity. Research, design and construction had to proceed simultaneously so that novel processes might be introduced with the minimum of delay. Because the research team were thus involved in the design, pilot plant operation and commercialised introduction of new processes, there never was that remoteness from the day-to-day operations which characterises some research activities; and this helped the subsequent move of so many research people into management roles.

One research project which proved to be of great importance related to the development of an acrylic fibre. This began in Courtaulds after both Du Pont and Monsanto had already established their acrylic fibres on a commercial scale in the USA. ICI could no doubt have obtained a licence under the Du Pont patents to manufacture their acrylic fibre, Orlon, in the UK or might alternatively have arranged for British Nylon Spinners to do so, but they had decided to put their effort behind their polyester fibre, Terylene. The first reference to Courtaulds' acrylic project was made in a statement by the Chairman to the shareholders in July 1955. This development was undertaken entirely within Courtaulds' own research department, apart from a brief visit to look at a pilot plant run by American Cyanamid in 1956.

Doubts
The doubts about the company's future which became apparent during these years arose from earlier concentration

upon the cellulosic fibres, and the virtual exclusion of the newer synthetic fibres. All of Courtaulds' senior management at the time shared the belief that cellulosic fibres had passed the peak of their growth, although there were varying degrees of emphasis about the prospects for their future. Tariffs on the cellulosic fibres compared quite well with the protection afforded in the UK to other textiles and in general with the protection afforded in other developed countries. However, threats of dumping, derived from rapid expansion of productive capacity in other countries combined with an expected reduced demand in export markets for cellulosic staple, led the man-made fibre producers to say in a joint memorandum presented to the Board of Trade in December 1955 (in connection with the Geneva tariff negotiations) that 'the future indeed is dark.' Earlier prosperity had resulted in too large a growth in capacity in the UK industry and there was severe price competition.

Attitudes within Courtaulds towards nylon and Terylene, the synthetic fibres which had already achieved successful commercial development, were influenced by the progress made by ICI in the UK and by the sight of Courtaulds' European competitors—AKU in Holland, Glanzstoff in Germany, CTA in France, with rights to manufacture under the respective patents regarding these fibres as the bulwark of their future expansion plans. ICI were new to the fibre industry; the others were the companies with which Courtaulds had always compared itself and regarded as its peers in the international man-made fibre world. In the USA, too, there was a common belief in the decline of the cellulosic fibres; Du Pont, for example, had abandoned viscose rayon staple manufacture.

It is not surprising, therefore, that attitudes towards the cellulosics were ambivalent, as suggested in the Chairman's statement to shareholders in 1956:

We estimate that the synthetics now comprise about ten per cent. of the world production of all man-made fibres, compared with roughly eight per cent. in 1954. There is a growing interest in these synthetics, more particularly on the American continent, where much progress has been made and where several producers now compete with each other for the available business. Progress has been somewhat slower in Europe, partly perhaps because of climatic conditions, but also because the average European is more conservative than his American counterpart in trying something new—especially so when he continues to be well served by the use of fibres with a cellulose base.

Courtaulds had indeed a 50 per cent interest in British Nylon Spinners under the terms of the Nylon Co-operation Agreement with ICI of 5 January 1940, and as an investment this was showing good results both in terms of the dividends which were distributed and the expansion plans which were under way, all financed from the nylon company's internal cash flow. Courtaulds invested no further cash after their initial investment of £4M (which can be compared with the value of about £130M placed upon their half share when they finally sold it to ICI in 1964). However, Courtaulds' management had no close involvement in the affairs of British Nylon Spinners. The senior directors who represented Courtaulds on the Board of that company kept all information very much to themselves and the expansion of nylon offered no scope for the ambitious in Courtaulds; this was already pre-empted by the established and independent management team at BNS.

Although there were doubts generally about the future for cellulosics, viscose rayon staple was seen as the fibre in this family which offered the most hopeful prospects. But some 30 per cent of the UK sales of viscose staple were made to the Lancashire spinning industry, and there were even greater doubts about the long-term viability of this market, because of its weak competitive strength in relation to some overseas producers. These sales to Lancashire made an important contribution to profits. In the manufacture of rayon staple the fixed costs which are independent of the volume of output represent a high proportion of total costs. So the loss of a part of the market would have a disproportionate effect on profits. If the Lancashire market were to disappear, profits would be reduced to substantially less than half their former level.

These doubts were expressed publicly by the Chairman in his statements to shareholders in 1955 and 1956. There began at this time in the industry a preoccupation with government policy in relation to textile imports from low wage-cost Far East sources, which sets the theme for much of the later relations between Courtaulds, the industry and government.

The prospect of British entry into the European Common Market was also viewed with trepidation. Thus an internal report dated 2 November 1956 states:

From the point of view of its own profits the company cannot welcome the prospect of a Common Market except perhaps as an extremely long-term proposition . . . the dangers for the company of the UK remaining outside the Common Market are also considerable, although their impact is more difficult to assess. Hence to oppose more discussion of terms between UK and European countries would clearly be politically inexpedient now that HMG appear in some degree committed to such discussions; opposition from Courtaulds might well be regarded as a natural reaction of a monopoly concern to the prospect of its monopoly disappearing. Opposition by the industry as a whole might be regarded as a proclamation of inefficiency unless backed by stronger supporting evidence than is now available.

The writers then considered the safeguards which the man-made fibre industry might seek, recognised that safeguards were inadequate, considered the defensive steps which the company might take and concluded that there was a need to examine investment prospects outside the textile field. This gloomy report was received by the Board without particular comment.

It is not until 1960 that a more robust attitude begins to appear. Thus the Chairman in July of that year said:

I have watched hopefully the developments in Europe. I well realise that the ECM and the EFTA involve changes that cannot be made without disrupting some well-established channels of trade. I also appreciate the political problems. Nevertheless as an industrialist I sincerely hope that HMG and the other Governments involved will find solutions which will lead to this country being in far closer trading relations with all the other countries of Europe, the Six as well as the Seven, so that the industry of this country may take part in the overall expansion which will result.

COMPANY POLICY TOWARDS TEXTILES

There had been some desultory examination of textile industry problems. Even in April 1938 two directors are quoted by Professor Coleman[2] as saying that Courtaulds 'had a mission to fulfil in teaching Lancashire how to modernise its methods.' On 12 May 1955 the Board discussed the 'diminishing tendency in the textile trade reflecting a fall-off of export business' and appointed a Committee to survey and report to the Board upon the position in the textile weaving industry in the UK.

Its report in July 1956 contained a clear analysis of what was happening and what might be expected 'looking into the future (i.e. 1966–70).' It was concerned only with the UK production of woven fabrics; knitting at that time was neither significant enough nor presenting problems large enough to be mentioned. There had been a reduction in UK output of woven cloth since 1951, primarily because of a loss of export markets. This decline was considered to be due to uncompetitive prices and to quality and styles being inferior to those of European and US competitors. Imports might be expected to increase if the industry were slow to put its house in order and if the government pursued its policy of trade liberalisation. In the short term, the report advocated marginal cost selling both by Courtaulds as yarn and fibre suppliers and (hopefully) by the UK users of fibre.

Taking a longer view, it was necessary for the industry to achieve the right structure and to employ better personnel. More intensive use of capacity would mean eliminating inefficient spinners and weavers. It was necessary to build up a sense of confidence without which technological progress would be impossible. The fixed selling price arrangements amongst some of the users of the company's products were preventing the needed changes, and should be brought to an end. It was advocated that Courtaulds should compete

2 Coleman, *Courtaulds*, vol 2, p 370.

vigorously, and increase its vertical links to achieve the more rapid development of new ideas. But the Board decided that these recommendations should not be accepted, for reasons not now discoverable.

A second Committee was established by the Board at its meeting on 12 December 1957 with much the same terms of reference. In January 1958 it considered a memorandum from the trade associations concerned putting forward a scheme for rationalising the cotton and rayon weaving industry. Neither the Committee nor the Board appears to have taken any lively interest in this scheme.

In 1957 Courtaulds had acquired British Celanese (see page 28) and by June 1958 the Committee seems to have become diverted into considering matters of secondary importance and was concerning itself with reorganising the Courtaulds/ Celanese weaving and knitting facilities.

By May 1959 the Committee was looking at details such as 'the future of the Spondon Print Works;' by November 1959 it was agreed that the meetings arranged for November and December would not take place and that in future 'a meeting should be called as and when there are items of business that require attention.' In 1960 the Committee was still in existence and was looking at proposals about some of the Celanese weaving mills; and a memorandum in January 1961 suggests, having reviewed the comparative failure of the government reorganisation plan for dealing with the dyeing and finishing industry, 'The Committee may care to consider whether there is anything which Courtaulds can do in this situation to give a lead to the industry.' Nothing further is recorded.

COURTAULDS' DEVELOPMENTS IN TEXTILES: 1957–62

From 1957 onwards a more active spirit is apparent. To provide a bench-mark against which to measure the company's subsequent development, it is useful to consider the key statistics relating to the year which ended on 31 March 1957.

Sales	£112M
Capital employed	£140M
Profits before tax	£15M

The employed capital incorporated a substantial proportion of new assets. In the ten years to 31 March 1956, the parent company's investment in fixed assets totalled some £44M, its investment in subsidiary companies about £20M, and its investment in associated companies about £6M—a total of £70M in all. In the same period the subsidiary companies had themselves retained profits of some £17M for development and expansion.

The profit figure represented the midway point in what was to prove to be a declining trend from the peak of £19M in 1954–55, falling in successive years to £18M, £15M and £13.5M.

The important elements in the more active phase which began in 1957 consisted in the rationalisation of the UK viscose filament yarn industry, the acquisition of British Celanese, the development of the acrylic fibre, Courtelle, and the diversification programme. Each of these had its influence on subsequent developments and therefore requires some explanation.

It is worth noting, however, that this more active phase was still essentially inward-looking, concentrating on strengthening the company's position in the UK cellulosic fibre market so far as possible, accepting that the future for the cellulosics was full of uncertainties and looking to diversification for growth. The acrylic fibre development (mentioned earlier) to be described in Chapter 3 was pursued on pilot-plant scale and confidence in its prospects grew as it became apparent that the process which had been developed had an inherently lower cost structure than that of the competitive acrylic fibres. Otherwise the environment which was brought within the focus of management attention was a limited one, and certainly for some years excluded the wider textile (fibre-using) field, as is demonstrated by the foregoing account of the work of the internal committees on this subject.

A major factor in explaining this emphasis was the personalities and stage of development of the key individuals concerned. The Celanese merger, the acrylic fibre development and the diversification programme were very much the personal responsibility of Mr C F (later Lord) Kearton. He had been appointed to the Board only in 1954 at the age of forty-three and it is remarkable (because so unusual) that even at this early stage he was having so much influence. To have expected him to have had even more influence and power at this stage in his career would have been unrealistic, especially when more senior directors had clearly looked at and decided against any involvement in the textile industry—the obvious area in which (with the benefit of hindsight) a more active policy might have been expected.

Viscose rationalisation

Courtaulds' success with viscose filament textile yarn in the 1920s tempted about thirty other firms into rayon production (including a few in acetate). Some were unsound from the beginning. Others did not survive the slump of the early 1930s. By 1934, apart from Courtaulds only six viscose producers survived. These disappeared as independent entities in various ways, mainly by Courtaulds acquiring them. They are listed below in order of size:

> British Enka—acquired by Courtaulds in 1961.
> Harbens—acquired by Courtaulds in 1959.
> Kirklees—acquired by Courtaulds in 1962.
> North British Rayon—closed down in 1956.
> Breda Visada—acquired by British Enka in 1952.
> Lustrafil—ceased production after fire in 1961; acquired by Courtaulds in 1963.

Courtaulds thus acquired the whole of the UK viscose filament yarn production capacity. It was already the only viscose rayon staple producer. Production was rationalised by closing down uneconomic plants, including the Courtaulds factory at Aber in North Wales in 1957.

British Celanese

The possibility of a merger with British Celanese had been first aired in 1936 when the two companies were engaged in prolonged and expensive patent litigation (which ended in 1937). Discussions about a possible merger continued in a desultory manner until 1940 and tentative approaches took place again in 1943 and in 1946. When the idea was raised again in January

1957 there was a fairly immediate response from the Celanese side and agreement was reached in April of that year. Why was it possible so quickly to agree in 1957 when nothing had happened in the previous twenty years? The Celanese profit record supplies a sufficient answer:

1953–54	£4.1M
1954–55	£3.3M
1955–56	£2.4M
1956–57	£1.6M
1957–58	£0.7M

The Celanese Chairman in his statement in 1956 had said, 'The main cause of our reduced profits has been a rapid and continual increase in costs which owing to intense competition in the industry we have not been able to recover by increased prices.'

The Celanese acquisition was substantial in the context of the Group's size at that time. The Courtaulds' offer had a market value of £19.5M, which can be compared with the value of the Group's employed capital at the end of March of that year of £140M. The basis was laid for a substantial improvement in profits. Costs were reduced by substantial reductions in the numbers employed, some of the disruptive price competition was removed (although Lansil remained as an independent aggressive competitor), and the newly developing triacetate fibre was successfully marketed.

There was a longer-term significance in the Celanese acquisition in that it brought with it interests in weaving, knitting, dyeing and finishing and garment-making. Although not a major reason for the acquisition, these wide-ranging interests provided a toehold in new fields such as garment-making, and an extension of the company's stake in others. This also meant that there were individuals whose experience could be helpful, and this increased confidence in managing some of the new activities.

These Celanese textile interests were associated with an approach to the marketing of fibres which was quite different from that of Courtaulds. Even in the 1920s Celanese were selling their own branded underwear woven and made up at their Spondon works. As Professor Coleman writes: 'In contrast with Courtaulds' staid and solemn advertising, these Celanese products were directed at the final consuming public with a flair for the fashions of the 1920s.'

Courtaulds had their long-established filament weaving business and a small warp knitting business, but this addition in 1957 of new textile activities gave an impetus which proved important in the development of the post-1962 years. Celanese had also a small pilot plant for the manufacture of nylon 6 (similar for most practical purposes to the nylon 66 made by British Nylon Spinners) which also played an important part in later developments.

THE COURTAULDS DIVERSIFICATION PROGRAMME

In December 1956 at the same time that the report on the Common Market was suggesting investment outside of the textile field, the research director in his own 'List of matters of high policy' included diversification as the least urgent 'but only if it is feasible and profitable.' He regarded as more important resisting the inroads of nylon in the tyre yarn field, dealing with the impending insolvency of the Canadian and Australian companies, achieving better prices for the cellulosic fibres, getting bigger dividends from British Nylon Spinners and successfully launching the acrylic fibre.

Despite the low priority which he attached to diversification, he gave reasons for recognising the need which seem singularly negative in contrast with later strategy. He considered that expansion in the man-made fibre industry would be slow, with exceptions not likely to benefit Courtaulds, that despite this the company must expand since otherwise it would lose its impetus and it would be impossible to maintain the forward-looking spirit necessary even to keep the company in the position it then held. Expansion in the man-made fibre industry could only be achieved through amalgamation with other companies. He saw no prospect of entering new fields through making major discoveries. However, the well-staffed research department 'is a very valuable asset which we are in danger of wasting unless it can find some major new problems upon which to work.' He concluded that the best prospect would be to buy up other companies capable of expansion. Investments in them would have to be 'of the order of tens of millions of £s.'

This was followed by a Board decision in January 1957 that 'In future Mr Kearton should be responsible for instituting enquiries into the possibility and desirability of the company diversifying its activities into cognate industries.' In November of that year one of the directors (Mr George Courtauld) was advocating 'A small nucleus of staff to collect and sift ideas' and 'A director of Courtaulds to give much of his time and to be responsible for diversification to the Board.' Diversification, he said, cannot be a side issue for a busy man whenever he may have a spare moment. The Board decided in November 1957 to appoint such a small group and a team was set up in January 1958.

This team's work in the following two to three years provided the major effort to diversify the firm's activities. In addition, however, there were other efforts such as those of the chemical research team which studied a possible petro-chemical complex and the technical and economic aspects of a number of possible new activities such as glass-fibre car bodies. In the USA there was a parallel but smaller scale effort of which the only concrete result was the acquisition of a 5 per cent shareholding in the Koppers Company as a way of fostering relations to discover whether there would be scope for common action with them; but this shareholding was sold after about two years when it became clear that there was no such scope. In Canada, local management initiated three small diversification projects of which two were failures and the third, a small carpet manufacturing company, has had only a modest success. In looking at the whole of this effort in retrospect it is chastening to consider the vast gap which can sometimes exist between effort on the one hand and results achieved on the other.

The paint industry was considered by the diversification team to be attractive. Although competitive, profits generally represented 15 per cent or more of invested capital in both large and small companies, and the Group's technical and research facilities could be deployed because of the new raw materials becoming available. Celanese had installed at Spondon the first oil-cracking plant to be established in the UK. This was primarily for the production of raw materials needed in the manufacture of acetate fibres, but there was a wide range of by-product chemicals, capable of being extended to provide raw materials for the paint industry. Courtaulds' financial strength could be used to foster the grouping together of existing firms which would be needed.

The first move was to acquire a small paint company at a total cost of about £640 000 in 1958. This was followed by the acquisition of Pinchin Johnson Limited in 1960 for a consideration which had a market value of £16.5M. Later still, in 1968, this by now sizeable paint company was further expanded by the acquisition of The International Paint Company, on terms which placed a value of £21.5M on that company. Thus Courtaulds eventually became one of the leading paint manufacturing groups, earning profits of £3.5M to £4M a year, in the UK and overseas.

Packaging was also considered a suitable investment area, because American experience and research in the UK suggested that expenditures on packaging were likely to increase at about twice the rate of growth in national income. Packaging involves the conversion of a number of basic materials—paper, board, tin plate, aluminium, plastics, glass —and employs numerous technologies. The Group already had know-how in the manufacture of transparent cellulose film, plastics and wood pulp and, finally, despite the existence of Metal Box and the Reed Group, there were a number of firms of medium size which were significant in the industry and might be suitable targets for acquisition. An initial investment of just over £2M was made in acquiring three companies, of which the most important was Reads of Liverpool. They had made arrangements with the American Can Company to manufacture open-top cans in the UK market in competition with Metal Box (whose know-how derived from Continental Can, the other large US producer of open-top cans).

The Group already had certain plastic interests as a by-product of acquiring British Celanese. These were extended by acquiring the right to manufacture Lego bricks in 1959, and by the acquisition in the same year of National Plastics Limited. The latter company had tax losses, and the net cost of acquisition proved to be negligible. One of the packaging companies, Betts, was also concerned in the use of plastics, and these activities together now represent an important part of the Celanese company.

The steel tyre cord project derived from observing the success of the steel tyre in the French market and judging that the same factors would eventually lead to a similar development in the UK at least in the truck tyre field. Michelin, the successful company in France, made their own steel tyre cord. There was an independent commercial producer in Belgium, but this was a family business and there seemed no prospect of negotiating with them. In the UK, British Ropes had a small experimental pilot plant and this was acquired (British Ropes retaining a minority shareholding). It became the nucleus for technical development work and capacity expansion.

The glass fibre and fabric project was inspired by the success of glass fabrics in the USA, and the comparative slowness in their development in the UK. Courtaulds had relations with United Merchants & Manufacturers in the USA; they were customers for Courtaulds' viscose rayon staple, but they were also large weavers of glass yarn. They had developed a small plant for the manufacture of glass fibre, and were thus the only company which could offer know-how in both the manufacture of glass fibre and of glass fabrics. Arrangements were made for a joint company, which acquired a small family business engaged in the weaving of glass fabrics; and this became the nucleus for the moderately successful Marglass Limited.

Despite the efforts which went into this experiment in diversification, it was becoming clear by about the middle of 1961 that a company of Courtlands' size was unlikely to be able to take on and manage a sufficient number of such projects to have a marked effect on the company's prospects. The view was beginning to be expressed that the firm should seek its future through becoming more deeply engaged in the UK textile industry, despite the difficulties. This was a revolutionary attitude in the context of past attitudes within the firm.

Lessons of experience

The chief lessons which were learned related to management. First, good managements are not generally available to be taken over, and although able individuals may come with an acquisition policy, direction and leadership must be provided from the outset. Secondly, the talents in Courtaulds required to do this might as well be applied to a large target as to a small one, and the limited energy and skill which is available can easily be dissipated. Thirdly, each type of business has its own special needs which those brought up in that line of business learn to cope with almost instinctively, but which can be acquired only slowly and painfully by newcomers, however able. Thus the scope for moving management from one field to another is limited.

Other things also became clear—that the targets have to be realistic in relation to the size of the market (there was no room for two companies like Metal Box), that growth does not itself improve the prospects of profit but that some position of competitive strength needs to be achieved for this, whether based on technology, marketing or priority in the field or any other way of tempering the impact of competition.

A bolder attack on a few big targets might have changed the face of Courtaulds to a degree which would have made diversification an adequate answer to the Courtaulds problem; but at this stage in the company's history nobody was ready for such a policy.

RELATIONS WITH ICI

Following the agreement in 1940 setting up British Nylon Spinners as a jointly owned company with ICI, there were further talks in 1943 concerning possible closer working relations between Courtaulds and ICI, including the possibility of a merger. Nothing came of these talks, and it was finally agreed that the two companies would each go their own way and neither would be inhibited from embarking on expansions in areas which might formerly have been considered the preserve of the other. The BNS collaboration necessarily called for continuing contact, and Courtaulds were of course

B

major customers of ICI for chemicals (especially caustic soda) and dye-stuffs.

ICI's decision in 1950 to embark on the manufacture of Terylene provoked discussion about whether this should be within the ambit of BNS, but this foundered on ICI's insistence that Courtaulds would then have to accept a minority position in BNS.

In 1960 the then Chairman of ICI wrote a memorandum about the frictions which existed in relations between the two companies. He instanced ICI's dissatisfaction with the profits which they received on supplying BNS with its basic raw material, Courtaulds' arrangements to acquire a competitive raw material manufacturing process from Italy, the competition between viscose and nylon in the tyre yarn market, and Courtaulds' diversification activities which were leading them into areas competitive with ICI. His conclusion was that there should be a complete merger of the two companies.

The then Chairman of Courtaulds, in reporting his conversations to the Board in October 1960, said, 'I believe that unless a satisfactory alternative solution can be found we should decide to negotiate on the basis of a complete merger.' The reaction of the Courtaulds' Board was distinctly lukewarm. It was recorded that the Board was opposed to a merger, that the Chairman should so inform the Chairman of ICI, and that when doing so he should add that 'in the view of the Board of Courtaulds problems and frictions between the two companies could and should continue to be settled with goodwill on both sides by dealing with them as and when they arose.'

Further discussions took place in the latter part of 1961. These were interrupted by a dramatic offer from ICI to the Courtaulds' shareholders which was subsequently increased. After a major public battle, ICI finally obtained no more than 38 per cent of the share capital of Courtaulds. This unstable situation was resolved in 1964, when Courtaulds' capital was reduced and ICI's shareholding cancelled. ICI acquired Courtaulds' 50 per cent share in BNS, and Courtaulds decided to go ahead with their own independent nylon project.[3]

[3] It is hoped that these events will be dealt with more fully in a third volume of Professor Coleman's history.

The failure of the ICI bid to acquire Courtaulds was the direct result of a realignment of forces within Courtaulds, provoked by the bid situation. The then Chairman had already in 1960 declared himself in favour of a merger. The Chairman-designate had given his colleagues the impression that he too saw no alternative to the company being acquired by ICI. In most circumstances this attitude on the part of the two most senior members of the Board would have been decisive. But the terms initially offered by ICI were poor and had to be opposed, and this gave an opportunity to those who were less committed emotionally than their two senior colleagues. If the final ICI terms had been offered at the beginning there could have been no argument.

To seize the opportunity to resist an unwelcome and inadequate offer it was necessary for those who felt most strongly to take charge of the situation, and since their views were shared by most of their colleagues there was no resistance to their doing so. It was natural therefore that when the immediate crisis was over these same individuals should continue to take charge, especially with the disappearance from the scene of the Chairman and his designated successor. In this way the management team which handled the post-1962 development of the business was able to begin with a relatively free hand, with the early departure of their more senior colleagues and the prestige which accompanied the success in battle. C F Kearton was and remained the dominant individual in this situation.

SUMMING UP

By the end of 1961, therefore, Courtaulds had a dominant position in the UK in the cellulosics field and only the small Lansil acetate plant was not under their control. However, the prospects were seen to be limited apart from possible new developments in improved types of viscose rayon staple. Hopes in this direction were qualified by doubts about the viability of the important Lancashire market. Courtaulds had explored the diversification route, and had come to the conclusion that it could not be sufficiently effective. The negotiations with ICI had been so handled that the possibility of an agreed merger with that company was excluded for some time to come. The fragmented textile interests had been brought under closer control following the Celanese merger, but no policy had been formulated for dealing more generally with the problems of the UK textile industry or for defining Courtaulds' role within it.

The management team which had emerged to take responsibility for the next phase in the company's development was peculiarly the product of these experiences in the 1950s. They had all been with Courtaulds for fifteen years or more by 1962, and so the company's successes and failures in these years had formed their attitudes—more particularly, of course, the successes and failures in which they had been concerned personally. It is impossible to know how differently a new management team from another environment might have behaved. But for these individuals the experiences which counted were those gained from the Celanese acquisition, the diversification episode, the ICI affair, the earlier management style which took pride in a gentlemen's club atmosphere; and the feeling of being on the brink of disaster for a long time. Their inheritance was a special one.

The policies which a manager pursues, and the methods and the style he adopts to carry them through, are thus in a state of constant development; and they are a consequence of what has gone before in his experience. What he does now is quite different from what he would have done ten years ago. Those not able to adapt and develop are unlikely to be the survivors who would deal with situations of the kind with which this study is concerned, and the outsider's view of how business is conducted may not always give sufficient weight to this evolutionary process.

Chapter Two

SOME TEXTILE INDUSTRY CHARACTERISTICS

Although the ICI affair was from one point of view the catalyst which brought a new management group into prominence in Courtaulds, its outcome represented from another viewpoint the elimination of one possible strategy. Because of the way in which events had been handled, a merger between Courtaulds and ICI appeared to be most unlikely for a long time.

Other possibilities had already been eliminated. A future based wholly upon fibres was ruled out because of the company's exclusion from nylon and Terylene; the later success of the new acrylic fibre was too distant at this time to be seen as a possible nucleus for company growth. Diversification had been tried and found inadequate. The post-1962 development of Courtaulds as a vertical fibre-textile group, mainly UK based, can thus be seen as a bid to survive as an independent business in a situation in which the alternatives had, one by one, been eliminated. A move forward into textiles was the only course which was seen still to be open. It was a challenge which met the needs of the management situation.

The next two chapters describe the actions taken and the methods used to carry through the verticalisation policy, and these set the scene for considering the interactions between Courtaulds and the government, which are the main theme of the study.

However, the directions in which Courtaulds moved initially in their verticalisation policy were dictated by those features of the textile environment in the UK of which the management was then conscious, although they did not have that detailed knowledge and feel of the situation which comes from actually being engaged in the trade. Some of those features were identified in the mid-1950s and were referred to in the previous chapter, but at that time they did not influence management thinking in any active way. This chapter is concerned, therefore, with the increasing awareness of the external situation which contributed to the course of events described in the next chapter.

As senior management saw it, the textile environment had four main characteristics: the slow overall growth in final demand; rapid structural and technological change giving possibilities of rapid growth in some areas and decline in others; increasing capital intensiveness; and government policies which permitted a high level of imports in association with uncertainty about their future trends. Any new company policy had to recognise these characteristics, if possible turn them to Courtaulds' advantage, and to accept the constraints which they imposed.

SLOW GROWTH WITH RAPID CHANGE, AND THE NEED TO ADAPT

During the 1962–72 period with which this study is mainly concerned, the UK domestic market offered a potential for sales of natural and manmade fibre products of about £2000M a year at manufacturers' prices, of which the fibre content has accounted for about £450M. Overall growth has been modest, however. Expenditure on textiles seems to increase at about the same rate as GNP, although the increase in volume has been greater because clothing prices have been declining relatively to other prices by about 2 per cent per annum.

But within the overall total, major developments were occurring by the 1960s. The share of man-made fibres in total fibre consumption had increased by some 8 to 10 per cent per annum and accounted for 36 per cent of the total in 1962, with every prospect of continuing to rise. Use of the cellulosics (viscose and acetate) was expanding less rapidly than that of the synthetics (nylon, polyester, acrylic). Man-made fibres were now competing with each other as well as with cotton and wool, with a high degree of interchangeability between them.

There were some interesting variations in acceptance for different end-uses, influenced not only by fashion whims but by resolute marketing techniques. For example, after initial difficulties in gaining acceptance in the 1930s acetate fibres established a market in the UK and in North America, especially for some types of underwear fabric with qualities of comfort and a luxuriant feel, but not generally in the manufacture of lining fabrics where the greater strength and abrasion resistance of viscose was advantageous. In Canada, however, the acetate yarn producer, competing with Courtaulds as viscose yarn producer, established a vertical operation in the 1950s which was technically no different from what anybody else was capable of doing; but by skilled marketing and pricing policies he was able substantially to eliminate viscose linings from the Canadian market.

In the 1950s too were developed the modified triacetate fibres which could be handled to give colour and texture characteristics suitable for fashion outerwear, and their use expanded rapidly in North America and the UK. In Canada, however, the acetate producer again established a unique position, through building up a carpet manufacturing business using triacetate and, again through skilled marketing, achieved a considerable success with a fibre which those most concerned at the time with its successful development elsewhere dismissed as completely unsuitable.

The supply of reinforcing material for tyre manufacture provides a similar story of changing fibre characteristics and interchangeability. Before 1940 all tyres were made with a cotton reinforcing fabric. During the war a superior, stronger viscose fibre was developed and by 1950 had more or less completely displaced cotton. In the early 1950s in the USA, nylon's success in the stocking market (because of its strength) was the basis for an attempt—in part successful—to capture the tyre yarn market. But nylon had certain inherent technical disadvantages well recognised by the car manufacturers who specified original equipment tyres. Thus, although the nylon glamour appeal achieved results in the replacement tyre market, the competitive position of the two fibres for some years in the middle and late 1950s was influenced greatly by their relative cost to the tyre manufacturer, and this could be expressed conveniently in terms of the price/strength relationship.

Under this competitive pressure the strength of the viscose yarn was successively increased in stages to nearer its theoretical maximum (that of nylon was already at its maximum). So for some years viscose held its market position in the UK more successfully than it had in the USA, where the nylon attack had been earlier and had given a forewarning of what could happen. By the late 1950s the development of the radial tyre was beginning to change the position yet again because here viscose had inherent technical merits as compared with nylon. Meanwhile the successful development of steel reinforcement in Europe and polyester in the USA had introduced yet further competitive influences.

Traditional distinctions between some of the fibre-using activities were fast being eroded, in part by rapid changes in fibre characteristics such as these, in part by changes in technology in the fibre-using industries themselves. Thus knitted fabrics were beginning to displace woven fabrics in many uses. By 1962 warp-knitted nylon fabrics had captured 15 per cent of the men's shirt market. Tufted carpets were accounting for 40 per cent of the carpet market. Since man-made fibres were predominant in the tufted sector this had important implications. The growth had been more than twice as fast as in the rest of Europe, though in the USA tufted carpets accounted for 85 per cent of the market. The texturising of filament yarns was beginning to eliminate the need for spun yarns for certain uses. Yarns of manmade fibres spun and woven on the cotton system were beginning to replace traditional suitings. By 1962 13 per cent of fibres spun on the 'cotton' spinning system were man-made. There were diverse movements in patterns of fibre consumption. For example, in 1950 rayon accounted for 70 per cent of fibre consumption in dresses, but this had been reduced to 40 per cent by 1957 when cotton had a fashion appeal. There was then a strong recovery in the triacetate filament form.

Changes in the distributive trades also were having noticeably important effects. The expansion of large retail chain stores and mail order firms was taking business away from the small independent retailers and diminishing the role of branded goods. The methods adopted by the expanding firms to organise the supply of goods to their required standards of quality led to manufacturing changes in the fibre-using activities. These were more concentrated in some types of products, such as children's wear and underwear, than in, say, household textiles and outerwear.

The fragmented structure of the textile manufacturing industry was thus becoming increasingly unsuitable for the requirements of the changing market elsewhere. Purchasing power was being concentrated in the large retailers down-stream and with relatively few man-made fibre suppliers upstream. Within the company the need was seen for similar concentrations in textile manufacturing to engage the increasing purchasing power of the large retail and wholesalers. Anything like comparable selling strength would require production and marketing economies. The new situation demanded more rapid larger scale responses by textile manufacturers to changing consumer needs, more rapid innovation as fibre and machine technology made more things possible, more uniformity of product quality and at a higher level, and the capacity in the fibre-using activities to bargain on more equal terms with suppliers and customers.

INCREASED CAPITAL INTENSIVENESS

The new technologies required heavy investment. In no broad sector of textiles production where four-shift working is common is investment per employee now lower than the UK manufacturing average (excluding textiles) of £4700. In man-made fibre production investment per head is in the range £10 to £20 000; and up to £10 000 for spinning, yarn texturising, weaving, warp and weft knitting. It was forecast that fixed capital per person employed in a fully integrated, new spinning, weaving and finishing mill running on three shifts with conventional equipment, could be £6000, about three times the then current average. To adapt to the new situation therefore required an ability to provide substantial cash sums for investment.

IMPORTS AND GOVERNMENT POLICY

In 1962 the Lancashire section of the industry (spinning and weaving on the 'cotton' system) was the main area of difficulty. Man-made fibres were still subject to tariffs which were relatively high, but the conclusion of the EFTA agreement in 1959 with its provisions for reducing tariffs had opened the UK market to new competition from fibre producers in Scandinavia and Austria. By 1962 mid-year, the chief EFTA countries had cut tariffs against each other to 50 per cent of former rates.

Fabrics made from man-made fibres were also protected at reasonably high levels from non-preferential sources even after the 20 per cent reductions in most tariffs implemented by the UK (from November 1962) under the international round of GATT negotiations (the Dillon Round); but many of these fabrics were close competitors with cotton particularly in blends.

The Lancashire industry, traditionally based on cotton and accounting for only some 16 per cent of the total textile industry (in terms of net added value), was particularly important to a fibre producer like Courtaulds. It represented an important market for some fibres, potentially of even greater importance as a result of new technical developments in the fibre field, such as the modified viscose fibres with high moisture absorbency and comfort. Duty-free imports of cotton fabrics from Commonwealth countries under the Ottawa agreements of 1932 were increasing and were exacerbating the problems of adjusting to the loss of traditional export markets. By 1961, already 25 per cent of domestic consumption was imported from low-cost sources, largely duty free from the Asiatic Commonwealth, which then compared with about 5 per cent in the EEC over a tariff. The UK 'cotton' industry was the only one in any developed country with no duty protection against a major supplier. The quota restraints which the industry negotiated with the three major Asiatic Commonwealth suppliers at the turn of the decade, reserved for these the right to negotiate supplementary quotas if total imports should increase to the advantage of other suppliers at their expense. This encouraged HM Government to maintain the bilateral agreements which existed with some other suppliers and introduce a few *ad hoc* controls on some new ones.

Under the 1959 Cotton Industry Act (discussed in more detail in Chapter 5) nothing was done to strengthen the structure of the industry; and its ability to compete internationally had not been much improved. Some concentration was evident; there were 100 spinners and 450 weaving companies, half the pre-war numbers. However, over fifty years' output had shrunk by about 80 per cent to under 2000 million yards in spite of UK home consumption doubling and world consumption trebling. The UK share of world exports fell from 60 per cent in those fifty years to 8 per cent. When the Ottawa agreements were signed, Lancashire was exporting over 500 million yards to India alone, and thirty years or so later importing from India, Pakistan and Hong Kong almost equivalent quantities, a reversal of almost a thousand million yards. Employment in the industry had fallen over the fifty years from over 600 000 to about 150 000, numbers of looms from 840 000 to 150 000 and of spindles from 60 million to 12 million.

The evident failure of the 1959 Act to achieve structural change was bound to strengthen that body of opinion to which reference was made in the previous chapter which regarded the Lancashire industry as basically uncompetitive and therefore expendable, some because they saw the workers more usefully deployed in the newer and then more fashionable industries such as aircraft and electrical engineering, others because they saw the UK with its Commonwealth associations as having a duty towards less developed nations far beyond any contribution which other developed countries were willing to make.

Cheap imports of cotton fabrics were hampering not only the commercial development of woven fabrics based on man-made fibres. Because woven and knitted fabrics were becoming more interchangeable for many end-uses, cheap imports from low-cost sources of woven cottons were also having a discouraging effect on the domestic textile industry generally. The traditional barriers between the various sectors of the fibre-using industries were of diminishing significance.

The period was of course also characterised by falling prices for man-made fibres. Viscose staple and spun rayon yarn prices had dropped to about the same as cotton prices by 1960, whereas pre-war they had been double; and prices for other man-made fibres were also falling as a result of increased production.

Japan was the cause of a good deal of concern, then more than later a 'low cost' supplier of a wide range of textiles. The voluntary restraints agreed under the 1962 Commercial Treaty, in some cases continuing earlier controls, were negotiated as a *quid pro quo* for accepting the principle of non-discrimination under GATT, and followed the concerted approaches from all sectors of the textile industry together. In face of the apparent government predisposition to liberalise, it was argued that policy should be to treat the textile and clothing industry as one and regard it as wholly sensitive in relation to Japan. The long-term implications of trade relations with Japan worried the man-made fibre producers. Together they lodged a major study with the Board of Trade in September 1961, to keep the Japanese problem in view in the Board of Trade.

In Geneva negotiations were taking place for an international Long Term Agreement on cotton textiles. In the period up to 1962 considerable effort was concentrated to assess the negotiating positions to recommend to HMG for the successive GATT Rounds of tariff negotiations,[1] the European Free Trade Association negotiations of 1959 and the abortive bid for EEC entry. As a result of this work there developed an increased awareness within the company of its involvement in the industry and a greater awareness of the external situation. The memorandum submitted by the man-made fibre producers for the Dillon Round of 1960–61 was a most comprehensive statement of the facts affecting international trade in man-made fibres. It set out particularly the factors encouraging dumping on world markets and the threats

[1] Geneva 1947, Annecy 1949, Torquay 1951, Geneva 1956 and the 'Dillon' Round of 1962.

of indirect dumping through third countries. The difficulty was stressed of evaluating the comparative benefits of tariff concessions whilst the pattern of duties in Europe was undergoing rearrangements of which the outcome was uncertain.

The 1955 examination of the Lancashire industry problem within Courtaulds had not led to any immediate action, but the continuing troubled state of the industry, its increasing importance to Courtaulds as a fibre producer and the inadequacy of government policies on structural issues all combined to turn the company's attention to consider what strategy might be suitable. It was by this time realised that Courtaulds might take active steps to intervene to stop the decline of its most important customer. This naturally increased the likelihood of interaction between the company and government.

Chapter Three

A VERTICAL FIBRE–TEXTILE GROUP

THE FORMATION OF THE STRATEGY

At no stage was the objective of Courtaulds becoming a fully-fledged vertical group explicitly enunciated, and an account in retrospect of the development makes it all seem much more logical than it appeared whilst it was going on. The existence in the USA of large, multi-product textile groups such as Burlington Mills and J P Stevens, vertical in all but fibre-making, provided a model of which those concerned both in government and in industry were always conscious. They were aware also that, since despite high US wages and fibre costs and prices not markedly different from those in the UK, the US textile industry seemed able to make profits (albeit modest) with selling prices not much higher than those in this country.

Because the strategy was never explicitly enunciated, an account at this stage of the actions which were taken is likely to provoke questions which cannot be answered from the contemporary record. Looking back, and with the benefit of all the intervening experiences, however, a number of threads can be detected which might helpfully be brought to view at this point in the narrative.

The initial vertical moves were determined by the size of the profits which were being earned or which it was thought could be earned—from viscose, acetate, acrylic and (later) nylon fibres. The reasons for believing that it was not possible to continue, as most other fibre producers throughout the world did, solely as a fibre company varied from one fibre to another. The Lancashire moves were dictated initially by the need to ensure a continuing UK domestic market for viscose rayon staple, both for the types already on the market and the newer types which were nearing commercialisation. (Later the ownership of Lancashire-type spinning facilities also became important for producing acrylic spun yarns for the rapidly expanding weft-knitting business.) Courtaulds judged that vertical moves towards the Lancashire industry were essential if they were to have any hope of retaining an important fibre market.

Verticalisation as it affected the acrylic fibre was much more associated with the inadequacies of the existing market for dealing with a rapidly growing new fibre on an adequate scale. At the stage of spinning the fibre into yarns there was need for additional capacity. Existing users were expanding by acquisition and internal growth, but concentration could go so far as to make Courtaulds vulnerable to a switch of their business to the US fibre competitors. Moreover, the quality standards of some of the independent using firms were not good enough.

In the knitting industry itself, where the yarns were used for manufacture into garments, a vertical policy would also make it easier to promote the sale of Courtaulds fibre against the US competitors, especially through the rapid translation of new development ideas into commercial products. There could never be any question of selling a Courtaulds fibre if the customer had good reasons for wanting a competitor's product, but there was scope for knowing what was going on, adjusting to it, and persuasively influencing buyers when differences were marginal or illusory.

The verticalisation activities based on filament yarn were differently motivated. In some fields acetate and nylon fabrics could be interchangeable. The glamour appeal of nylon was leading users to switch temporarily from acetate because of high profit margins and, though this could not last, these markets once lost would be expensive to recover. Newer types of acetate yarns (triacetate) were ready for launching, and long experience with their own filament weaving and warp knitting businesses had shown Courtaulds' management the merits of speed in launching new products, and also how a vertical business could perform more effectively in this respect.

When later (in 1964) it was decided to embark on a new

independent nylon project it was obvious that at that late stage it would be expensive to break into the market held by competitors, and a vertical attack would have more chance of success. There can be much greater flexibility of attack on a competitor's position through competing with his customers in their own products, provided there is sufficient management and technological skill to feel sure that those customers have no inherent cost advantages.

The choice between acquisition and internal expansion as a way of becoming vertical is not susceptible to easy generalisations. In filament weaving and warp knitting the company had an established market position, a substantial share of the market and competent management, and government investment incentives provided a powerful reason to expand capacity by buying new equipment. As a way of obtaining physical capacity this is generally cheaper than acquisition, although generally not cheaper as a means of establishing a market position.

But in Lancashire spinning, Courtaulds had no established management, no special technological understanding or market position and the total market was stable or declining. Acquisition seemed the more sensible approach, even though substantial sums had then to be found to install modern equipment as a means of making the acquired business competitive by international standards.

The same considerations applied to Lancashire-type weaving. Yet it was decided not to acquire but to build and equip new plants. This was because the firms were mainly private companies and thus difficult to acquire by way of a takeover bid, and most of the buildings would have been unsuitable for modern equipment. One consequence of this choice was that the disappearance of the high-cost established firms was slower and more costly.

The market share at which Courtaulds were aiming in their verticalisation also varied according to circumstances. The UK market was generally regarded as the reference point for this purpose, but with a growing realisation that it was becoming less and less relevant as tariffs were reduced, and that it would become even less relevant with entry into the European

Common Market. In filament weaving and warp knitting, where there was a strong established position and where growth was mainly through internal capital expenditure, no particular targets were set. Expansions were considered by reference to the general growth in markets, especially the export opportunities, considerable in these areas because of the company's highly competitive cost position.

In Lancashire the company's one-third share of the market followed from the decision to acquire Fine Spinners and Doublers and the Lancashire Cotton Corporation, which together accounted for about this proportion. To acquire both was necessary to have any prospect of influencing government attitudes about imports. To acquire more would have been unduly hazardous—risks were being taken already—and difficult because there was little left that was worth acquiring in the spinning field, except in companies like Viyella and English Sewing Cotton whose boards would (at that time) have been unwilling to sell.

In the stocking field the aim to achieve about 30 per cent of the market was related to the offtake needed to operate a viable nylon business.

Although initially the vertical moves were closely related to individual fibres, later there was a more opportunist approach. This arose in part from management's growing confidence in its ability to handle any kind of textile activity. Also as the fibre-dominated moves were achieved it became obvious that nobody could foresee where the next developments would be. Man-made fibres were increasing their share of all textile markets. Courtaulds were successfully making and selling all of the established fibres with the exception of polyester, and it seemed sensible to extend on a broad front into the textile field if businesses were available on attractive terms.

The general approach was expressed by the then Chairman (Sir Dallas Bernard) in his statement to the stockholders in July 1964:

. . . the problem affecting one sector of the textile industry cannot be considered in isolation . . . As fibre suppliers to all sectors, with a range of activities covering every stage of manufacture, your company has an important contribution to make in realising the industry's potential in terms of growth and exports.

This statement was a pointer to the direction which company policy would take for some years to come.

DEVELOPMENT OF THE POLICY

As has been shown, the circumstances of each fibre were different and this influenced the moves towards verticalisation. The policy was initially related closely to the Group's fibre activities. Acquisitions were the means for extending into relevant markets. The three prominent strands were first, those acquisitions which can be identified with the viscose rayon staple business; secondly, those connected with the company's developing acrylic fibre business; and thirdly, those identified with the filament textile yarns, viscose, acetate, nylon from 1964 onwards and (much later) polyester.

The table indicates the relevant fibres and the salient facts about Courtaulds' involvement in them during the years with which this study is concerned.

The initial preoccupation with safeguarding fibre outlets was explicitly confirmed in the statement of the Chairman (Mr C F Kearton) in July 1965, with reference to viscose rayon staple and the Lancashire activities. In other fields the emphasis was slightly different:

The expansion of our interests in weaving and knitting, in dyeing and printing, in hosiery and garments, and in converting and merchanting have all been motivated by the wish to get closer to the ultimate consumer. We expect the individual enterprises to be properly profitable, of course, but we do place considerable value on the knowledge they bring us of the practical problems in converting our man-made fibres into consumer goods.

But the acquisition policy first followed routes closely related to fibre activities.

	1962	1971
	('000 tons)	
Viscose staple		
Production	110	160
Home deliveries	85	81
Share of UK market	95%	76%
Courtelle (acrylic fibre)		
Production	7	72
Home deliveries	4	39
Share of UK market	36%	47%
Filament textile yarns		
ACETATE		
Production	19	34
Home deliveries	15	22
Share of UK market	75%	73%
VISCOSE		
Production	27	18
Home deliveries	18	10
Share of UK market	95%	77%
NYLON		
Production	NIL	28
Home deliveries	NIL	21
Share of UK market	NIL	18%

The Lancashire strand

Courtaulds' recognition of the need for large vertical groups in the Lancashire industry was made the subject of general debate in the industry from mid-1962 onwards. The main requirements were seen as being:

1 Groups large enough to achieve production and marketing economies, which would imply a throughput of 100 million yards a year.
2 Vertical as between weaving and converting, preferably with dyehouse.
3 Each section of the Group responsible for its own profits and free to buy and sell outside the Group.

The first move after the ICI episode was the so-called Northern Plan which envisaged the merger into one group of The Lancashire Cotton Corporation (LCC), Fine Spinners and

Doublers (FSD), English Sewing Cotton (ESC), Tootals and Combined English Mills (CEM). This was a Courtaulds conception, but its launching within the industry followed meetings in November 1962 with senior Board of Trade officials who had indicated their belief in the need for major reorganisation. Officials saw that without major structural changes and the emergence of powerful groups, the traditional Lancashire textile industry had little chance of survival. They believed that the fibre producers were the natural people to take the initiative because Lancashire was such an important market for them. The initiative in approaching the fibre producers came from the government side. It was made clear that the government could not be expected to do more to help the industry, financially or by seeking agreement with exporting countries, unless the industry were seen to be doing more to help itself. Courtaulds felt encouraged by Board of Trade officials to take an initiative. The objective was to form a strong group which could effectively manage the troubled Lancashire section of the industry.

This plan, large in relation to the company's resources, was bold in the context of Lancashire's situation and of the government attitudes towards Lancashire referred to in the previous chapter.

A change of government policy towards some form of protection would be essential to viability. It was judged that such a change would be unlikely to follow any further complaint about the plight of the industry and pleas for help, but it might be expected to follow a demonstration that some of those involved in the industry were willing to back their judgement that a viable long-term future could be achieved. To that extent the Courtaulds' moves here described were a bold act of faith. As the Chairman said in July 1968: '... we do depend as we did when we started on our ambitious and far-reaching Lancashire plans, on a continuing constructive attitude from Her Majesty's Government.'

It was recognised that the companies included in the Northern Plan did not represent a logical grouping, being much too heavily weighted towards spinning (with a yarn output of some 150 million pounds a year); but it included Courtaulds' largest customers for viscose rayon staple, and would be a step towards safeguarding that market.

The scheme was first discussed with the Chairman of ESC with whom the 1960 discussions had been held. He saw no prospect of an ICI initiative and welcomed the Courtaulds' scheme, in part because Courtaulds' shares would offer a more powerful medium for enforcing change than was available to any Lancashire firm.

Private talks about the Northern Plan were making good progress and offers with a value of some £50M were envisaged. However, the Courtaulds' Board was persuaded in December 1962 that ICI, with their then 38 per cent shareholding in Courtaulds, should be informed. ICI wished to participate, though accepting that Courtaulds would have a majority. It took some time for the ICI directors to familiarise themselves with the situation, but a scheme agreed by the merchant bankers was finally presented to the chairmen of the five companies concerned in April 1963. It foundered because one of them, having accepted the valuation placed on his company as a result of the bankers' consultations, could not accept that valuation when he saw how it compared with the valuation placed upon his major rival. However, a process had been initiated which led to big changes.

Within a few weeks ESC made an offer to acquire Tootals, and negotiated loans from both ICI and Courtaulds, convertible into equity shares, which would give both ICI and Courtaulds a minority stake (thus incidentally complicating the task of any would-be takeover bidder, unless ICI and Courtaulds were acting in concert). CEM was acquired by Viyella. This left LCC and FSD, which Courtaulds acquired in August 1964. These, together with the smaller Hayeshaw company previously acquired, gave Courtaulds a 30 to 35 per cent share in the Lancashire spinning industry at a cost of some £40M, compared with Courtaulds' then employed capital of just under £240M.

Courtaulds' object here was to safeguard against import competition one of the important markets for both of the varieties of viscose rayon staple then in production, and also for the new polynosic types with which it was hoped eventually to capture for rayon some 20 per cent of the natural cotton consumption. The reasons were explained by the Chairman in his speech to stockholders in July 1965:

> We wanted to do our part to ensure that there would indeed be a Lancashire industry to take our man-made fibres in the future. We wanted to work directly with the industry to raise productivity, so as to ensure competitive power both in home and in export markets. It is our firm belief that the present state of technical knowledge allows cotton-type spinning, weaving and finishing to become capital intensive rather than labour intensive.
>
> It is clear that given the right investment, the textile industry can contribute more to economic growth than most other industries. But such investment depends on confident long-term planning. This in turn means that Lancashire must have some assurance, in the next few vital years, that the United Kingdom will not continue to be the world's dumping ground for cotton-type textiles. All other countries regard their domestic textile industries as vitally important to the general economic well-being. I have never been able to understand why some quarters seem so hostile to Lancashire's traditional industry, and are so ready to contemplate its decline. Common sense surely would urge that it is re-established, and revitalised.

Mere acquisition was not enough. It was necessary also to plan a major re-equipment programme if these spinning plants were to compete with the best of those in Europe. Re-equipment plans were put in hand immediately. By July 1965 eleven re-equipment schemes had been approved. It was planned to reduce the number of mills in operation from fifty to thirty-one, with an increase in capacity from 3.5 to 4 million pounds a week. (The way that Courtaulds organised itself to make all these decisions, and the many others described below, is discussed in full in Chapter 4.)

As a by-product of the acquisitions the Group now had a number of Lancashire-type weaving units—Frostholme, Burnley and Colne—small in total, however, when compared with the 30 per cent or so of spinning capacity within the

Group. It was necessary to do something more about Lancashire weaving, because this section of the industry was much
more fragmented than spinning and owned largely by private
companies not so susceptible to acquisition, and they were in
need of re-equipment for which existing buildings were unsuitable. Any re-equipment plans would require installation of
Sulzer looms, some of the most advanced in the market for
weaving a wide range of spun fabrics. A world map of the
Sulzer loom installations at the time is most revealing. There
were hardly any in the UK, whereas every other developed
country had several.

So it was decided to build on green field sites at Carlisle,
Lillyhall and Skelmersdale, taking full advantage of development area grants and other financial help. This meant that the
new mills would not be in the traditional Lancashire weaving
areas. But with a total planned capacity of 240 million yards a
year, they represented a major new factor in the UK market
since the comparable output from existing mills was no more
than 800 million yards. So the Courtaulds' plants could only
succeed if there were a substantial elimination of existing
capacity or a reduction in imports, or a combination of the two.

This aspect of the post-1962 development of the company
accounts for about 25 per cent of the new capital invested—
whether by acquisition (LCC, FSD, Hayeshaw and Ashton
Brothers in July 1968) or cash expenditure on new plant,
equipment and buildings—and it includes cash spent in extending and modernising the viscose staple facilities. The
moves into cotton-type spinning had given Courtaulds a 34
per cent share of the market by 1970, from virtually nothing
in 1962, and the spinning group's consumption of viscose
rayon staple accounted for about 20 per cent of domestic
sales of that product. The weaving activities had secured 10
per cent of the UK market, but only two-thirds or so of the
planned capacity was in use.

Although initially related mainly to the viscose staple
market (actual and potential) the Lancashire side of the post-
1962 development has subsequently made a major contribution to the development of an integrated acrylic fibre—weft
knitting business, as described overleaf.

The acrylic fibre strand

The second strand in the post-1962 development can be related to the successful commercialisation of the Courtaulds' acrylic fibre 'Courtelle'. The process developed by Courtaulds appeared to be very competitive. An aggressive investment in fibre manufacture was intended to pre-empt for Courtaulds a substantial share of the UK market, and capacity was increased in successive stages to 200 million pounds per annum. (The simultaneous, successful development of the French company is another story less closely related to the main theme, but relevant to management's current preoccupations and to plans for developing the company's business in the EEC— and in the context of these preoccupations the Whitehall interventions to be discussed later were an even greater diversion.)

The first stage in the marketing of this fibre consisted in its spinning into a yarn suitable for knitting or weaving. In the commercial development of cotton-spun yarns the company's involvement in Lancashire proved to be important. By 1970 the Spinning Division's activity and profits were heavily dependent on spinning acrylic yarns for the Group's weft knitting business, Exquisite Knitwear.

The other route, worsted spun yarns, presented problems because of the dominant position of Coats, Patons & Baldwins (Coats Patons) and their action further to strengthen that position by acquiring (100 per cent or partially) the other available spinners. Coats Patons were, of course, also buying fibre for spinning from competitors such as Du Pont, and in August 1967 Du Pont's price was reduced 20 per cent (18d.) overnight. The cost to Du Pont with their limited volume in the UK market was negligible in the context of their size and the potential at stake. Courtaulds' plans naturally envisaged price reductions of this magnitude and even more. Indeed they could never expect to sell the output for which they were planning capacity at the then prevailing prices. But the Du Pont reduction, which Courtaulds had to meet if they were to achieve the strong market position at which they were aiming, reduced profits by some £3M a year at an inconvenient time. Courtaulds decided on a new independent worsted spinning plant at Spennymoor where capital and training grants were available, employing former miners.

Courtaulds' competitive position was further enhanced as a result of a technical breakthrough. A method was developed of producing ready-dyed fibres (Neospun), giving fast colours more cheaply than standard dyeing techniques. In five years sales expanded from nothing to 44 million pounds a year. ICI had been thought to have achieved a major success as a result of expanding sales of their textured polyester fibre, the Crimplene process; yet Crimplene took ten years to achieve a growth similar to that of Neospun.

Acquisitions also played an important part in the establishment of Courtelle. The acquisition of Foister Clay & Ward and Bairnswear in 1963 represented the first substantial entry into the knitted garment industry, and the acquisition of Susan Small later in that year brought into the group Exquisite Knitwear, which was then minute: but it provided the basic technology and skilled staff in weft knitting for rapid expansion. The scale and speed of the subsequent expansion were enormous, with sales increasing from £3M in 1963 to £20M in 1970.

The Kirkland development is also relevant. This relatively small manufacturer of knitting machines (acquired as a by-product of the Gossard acquisition) had developed a double-knit jersey machine which was ready for commercial exploitation just at the moment when the market was beginning to expand. It thus became the natural supplier of weft knitting machines for Courtaulds' use and later exported them to the USA where the weft knit market development came later.

This acrylic-based second strand of the post-1962 growth accounted for about 15 per cent of the total investment, including acquisitions.

The filament yarn strand
The third strand in the post-1962 development relates in part to the established acetate filament yarn business, in part to the 1964 nylon project. Because the latter was initiated so late in the growth of nylon (see Chapter 1), Courtaulds aimed from the outset to secure a substantial internal market.

The needs of acetate and those of nylon together lay behind the expansion of the established filament weaving business—mainly from within but with minor acquisitions (including Nelson at the end of 1963). Earlier ideas to strengthen the filament weaving business had included discussions with English Sewing Cotton in 1959 and 1960 about a joint company which would incorporate Courtaulds' filament weaving interests. The objectives had been defined:

1   To be large enough to bargain with largest customers for converted cloth in equal terms.
2   To be large enough to achieve production and marketing economies.
3   To reduce financial risk by broadening the fibre or end-use pattern.

It was taken for granted that any new organisation would be largely vertical to give flexibility in pricing and to permit the rapid development of new ideas and products. The memorandum prepared jointly by officials of the two companies is quite clear about the main problem:

Fundamentally, the piecegoods selling industry has not developed selling strength comparable to the buying strength of its customers. As retailers become even more concentrated and independent and wholesalers combine in purchasing, this disparity will grow unless the textile industry takes action. . . .

Having examined the possibility of a merger which would embrace ESC and Courtaulds' filament weaving activities, it was decided that there was insufficient scope for improving profits through common management—insufficient 'synergy' to use the more recent jargon word—and the idea had been dropped, but both sides agreed that major amalgamations were needed and should be actively pursued. Thus it was suggested that an attractive group aimed at bigness, with a good balance of widespread interests, might be formed from ESC, Courtaulds' filament weaving business, Ashton Bros, Tootals and Carrington & Dewhurst.

There was indeed more common ground between Court-auld's filament weaving activities and those of Carrington & Dewhurst (C & D), and there were discussions shortly before those with ESC. C & D and Courtaulds together accounted for the greater part of the UK filament weaving industry, but there was intense competition and profits were poor; so in 1963 there were renewed conversations about a merger of the two companies' filament weaving activities. As before these foundered on the unwillingness of the C & D management to lose their independence and become involved in what they regarded as problems of the Courtaulds situation. It was agreed, however, that Courtaulds would buy a 10 per cent shareholding in C & D and appoint a representative to their Board, and that this would lead to closer collaboration. Then in November 1963, following an approach from ICI, the C & D Board agreed to give ICI a similar stake. In December both ICI and Courtaulds increased their holding, each buying 50 per cent of a large block of shares which was on offer. In November 1964 however, when it was proposed that Courtaulds should match ICI in investing yet further cash, the Courtaulds Board decided that the C & D management were not interested in serious collaboration, and so, although ICI increased their holding, Courtaulds did not. There were further abortive talks in 1967 about more far-reaching arrangements and the shares were finally sold in January 1968.

The Group's warp knitting activities based on the use of filament yarns were similarly expanded, including acquisitions such as the Derby & Midland company, though internal growth was the more important. Sales increased fourfold in the period under review. The acquisitions of Kayser Bondor, Clutsom Penn and Northgate were also part of this process. The last two were substantial users of nylon and it appeared at one moment as if ICI might counterbid, despite their policy of avoiding ownership of textile activities; but nothing happened and the Courtaulds offers succeeded. The needs of the nylon situation also dictated the stocking company acquisitions and their re-equipment with modern machines.

This third strand accounts for about 25 per cent of the new

investment in the decade, including acquisitions. The most important of these were:

		£M
James Nelson	Dec 1963	5.6
George Brettle	Jan 1964	0.6
Fras Hinde	Mar 1964	0.7
and	Jan 1965	0.2
Derby & Midland Mills	Oct 1965	2.3
Kayser Bondor	Jan 1966	2.5
Aristoc	June 1966	5.5
Ballito	Oct 1966	0.7
Symington	Aug 1967	1.8
Clutsom Penn	Feb 1968	17.7
Northgate	Mar 1968	10.5
Contour	Mar 1968	2.5

By 1970, as a result of acquisitions and internal growth, Courtaulds had 26 per cent of the UK filament weaving market, 40 per cent of the warp knitting market and 25 per cent of the stocking market; and sales to group users accounted for 60 per cent of domestic acetate yarn deliveries and 80 per cent of nylon deliveries. Verticalisation had developed from small beginnings, some in the more distant past, including especially the traditional filament weaving, the long-established warp knitting activities, and the textile activities (knitting and garment-making especially) which came with British Celanese.

Other verticalisation moves
Other strands in the post-1962 development included the acquisition of wholesaling businesses. In the year 1967–68 seven wholesaling companies were acquired for a consideration valued at about £13M and they were formed into a division 'of sufficient size to achieve benefits from rationalisation of buying and distribution.' This venture was part of the continuing effort to strengthen the company's position in relation to the rapidly changing retail scene. It was apparent that the disappearance of small retailers was due in part to the high costs of distribution through traditional wholesale channels, adding typically some 25 per cent to the cost of textile products between the manufacturing stage and their arrival in the hands

of the retailer. It seemed worth making some effort to achieve economies, and one way of doing this was to encourage bulk buying of manufactured goods from the company's textile range.

Courtaulds had an additional motive for the attempt because some of the acquisitions had brought well-established brand names into the Group and their future was prejudiced by the continued growth of the large retail chains at the expense of the smaller shops. Developments in the grocery trade had shown that something could be done to improve traditional methods of supplying these smaller units.

There were also acquisitions which extended Courtaulds' position generally in textiles without relating directly to any one of the main fibres. The most important of these were:

			£M
Morton Sundour Fabrics	Oct	1963	0.1
	and Feb	1965	0.2
Susan Small	Nov	1963	2.2
Victor Marks	Oct	1963	0.2
Meridian	Dec	1963	4.1
Barracks Printing	Mar	1964	0.2
Premier Dyeing	June	1964	0.5
Spray & Burgass	Dec	1964	1.2
Joseph Sunderland	Jan	1965	0.2
Samuel Heap	Jan	1965	0.2
Wolsey	June	1967	8.5
Morley	Jan	1968	1.5
Thomas & Arthur Wardle	Mar	1968	2.3
R Rowley	July	1968	0.7
Moygashel	Nov	1968	6.1
Fletcher	Sept	1971	0.8

These and other later acquisitions reflected management's growing confidence in their ability to handle textile activities, and a belief in the need to be broadly based in order to exploit whatever scope might arise for extending the market for man-made fibres of any kind, if made by Courtaulds.

ASSESSMENT OF THE VERTICALISATION POLICY

Throughout the whole period from 1962 onwards the Group's acquisitions received considerable publicity, especially when there was opposition, and this obscured the importance of the internal expansion which was going on; so in the statement of the Chairman (Sir Frank Kearton) in July 1969 a table was given to indicate the directions in which the company had moved in its investment activities in the years 1962–69.

	£M	£M
Acquisitions		
Fibre-making	9.3	
Fibre-using	145.9	
Other	20.7	175.9
Re-equipment and expansion		
Fibre-making	136.7	
Fibre-using	56.7	
Other	33.7	227.1
Total		403.0

As the Chairman had said in 1968: '. . . it is our re-equipment and internal expansion programme which is the more exciting for the future.'

Acquisitions were the route into new and less familiar parts of the fibre-using industries and the re-equipment and expansion in these areas played some part in justifying the large investments in fibre-making.

The degree of verticalisation reached by 1970 varied from one activity to another, and became progressively less with the activities nearest to the point of retail sale. Thus in 1969 when 37 per cent of Group home deliveries of fibres were made to Group companies, the garment activities accounted for only $3\frac{1}{2}$ per cent of this total, whilst wholesale and retail activities accounted for a negligible amount. The verticalisation process had consisted much more in the conversion of fibres into yarns and fabrics which had to be sold competitively to other textile manufacturers, and but little in the supply of products direct to the retail and distribution network, except in one or two special areas such as stockings and lingerie.

The Group which has emerged from almost a decade of active development is thus not a fully coherent, vertical fibre-textile business. A few dominant themes can be traced in its development—the need to safeguard or develop fibre markets, the need for size as such in dealing with threats from larger competitors, the growing power of the retailers enhanced by the fragmentation in many sectors—but the outcome is a patchwork, still capable of and requiring development. It reflects too the failure to carry through some of the acquisitions which might have been useful. For example the failure of the original Northern Plan has been mentioned. When in 1967 Viyella sought to acquire ESC (which would not have existed if the Northern Plan had been accomplished) the ESC–CPA (Calico Printers) merger was the defensive result. The single company that resulted—English Calico—was the subject of the Courtaulds bid in 1968 which led to the setting up of a Committee under the Rt Hon Edmund Dell (Minister of State at the Board of Trade)—one of the industry–government interactions to be considered later.

The Viyella situation is of special interest. The expansion of the Viyella business and its financial links with ICI form no part of this study. In 1966, however, there were intensive discussions about merging the textile activities of Courtaulds with Viyella into a company which Courtaulds would control, and later about a possible acquisition. Although these talks reached an advanced stage no agreement was concluded, and thus Viyella remained independent. Indeed the financial link with ICI was terminated. Courtaulds had also failed to come to any arrangement with C & D, and these two (Viyella and C & D) were thus the two major independent companies when ICI decided in 1969 to seek to acquire them; and this led to the setting up of a Committee under the Paymaster General, the Rt Hon Harold Lever—another of the industry–government interactions to be considered later.

The UK industry's net domestic sales in 1970 were about £2000M. Courtaulds' sales of textile products, other than for consumption in the industry, compare with those of other major UK textile concerns as follows:

	£M
Courtaulds	210
Carrington/Viyella	60
CPB	89
English Calico	50
Illingworth Morris	25

Thus Courtaulds accounts for little more than 10 per cent of the whole, and the largest five firms together account for about 20 per cent of sales outside the industry. Fragmentation downstream remains considerable. Excluding the five large firms already mentioned, the number of firms remaining in key areas of the industry in 1970 were as follows:

Cotton-type spinning	50
Weaving	230
Warp knitting	150
Weft knitting	160
Knitted garments	700
Made-up clothing	6000

This survey has concentrated upon the product and market strategies which led to the competitive battles which took place, and occasioned the proper concern of government in looking at the public interest. The impetus to it all sprang from the urge to see Courtaulds survive as an independent entity and from the more personal strivings of senior management towards fulfilment or self-justification which found their convenient focus in the struggle to make a success of Courtaulds. So it is necessary now to consider the effect of this activity on the business as a whole. The overall results provide the only valid test of performance within the institutional framework of a mixed economy system.

It will be recalled that some 20 per cent of the company's activities are outside the fibre-textile area and some 20 per cent are outside the UK; so although the changes described in this chapter have been the most important influence on the company's growth in the 1960s, the fibre-textile activities in the UK account for perhaps two-thirds of the Group's total activities. Yet for financial planning purposes, and in assessing performance and viability, the business must be viewed as a whole, and this is the reference point to which all management action must relate.

The interrelations between product and market strategies and financial strategy have been well described elsewhere (particularly in the publications of the Boston Consulting

Group, Inc.[1]) and for the present purpose it is necessary only to emphasise a few of the issues.

First, the use of the company's cash resources, whether from retained earnings or from new financing, reflects an assessment of future possibilities and has no connection with the sources from which the cash has derived. At a mature stage individual products supply far more cash than is needed to hold the market position which has been established. Initially any new project is a drain on cash resources which must have been provided from earnings on some more mature products, and the really difficult decisions are those relating to products which are believed to be at the take-off stage where large sums have to be provided in the hope of later profits, with running-in and initial losses which may continue for several years in the types of businesses with which this study is concerned. It is a fallacy to believe that each such new venture can be financed *de novo* on the basis of prospectuses assessed and backed (or not) by independent financial professional investors. This would mean rejecting the advantages of large-scale management for the sake of a theory, a course which none of our large industrial competitors would follow; indeed in Japan and Germany the internal financing of expansion is probably carried further than in the UK.

Second, the investment and pricing strategy for a new product at the take-off stage is designed to capture a large market share, because this provides the basis for low costs and selling prices. It is obvious that the judgement must be well founded and that there must be a real prospect of having costs substantially lower than competitors. The forecast is to some extent self-fulfilling if the large volume of output from a high market share is in fact achieved. Courtaulds' strategy with their acrylic fibre is an example of the successful use of these methods. Heavy borrowing to finance rapid expansion at a cost lower than the return which is expected on equity finance thus becomes an element in the marketing strategy; and Courtaulds' heavy borrowings in these years (it is now by UK standards a highly geared company) were a recognition of this truth.

[1] Industrial Pricing Policy and Strategy—Working Papers (London 1970).

C

As an index of management performance the record of these years is remarkable chiefly for the size and speed of the change which was brought about:

	£M	
	1962	*1972*
Capital employed	234.6	527.8
Sales	173.3	681.5

This chapter has sufficiently described the variety of directions in which this growth was achieved, and the combination of acquisitions and internal capital spending which provided the means; and the following chapter will describe the management methods which were used. It remains to put the process into the perspective which management would consider relevant.

First, as to profitability, the Chairman said in July 1966, in speaking of the textile activities:

The overall pre-tax return on capital of 10 per cent, is thus not yet up to the general standard of the Group. But some of the units in this complex are now producing over 15 per cent on the capital employed, and we intend to strive to see that the others are brought up to the level of the best. All this will take time.

It is taking longer than expected to reach this level of profitability. In the year 1971–72 the return on capital was 11.46 per cent. When compared with other large fibre producers, and in the context of generally depressed trading conditions for three years and worldwide excess capacity for the manufacture of man-made fibres, the Courtaulds results look remarkably good. There are a number of reasons for this, including Courtaulds' lesser dependence than others on profits from the nylon and polyester fibres which have suffered particularly. But the vertical structure of the Group has contributed too through enabling speedy commercial responses, tighter financial control and less scope for being played off against competitors.

From a longer-term point of view there have been repeated expressions of confidence in achieving better results, and because of its size and its power to respond the Group is now a more formidable rival to the large chemical companies which dominate the man-made fibre industry. Sales figures provide a rough and ready measure because they are an indicator of the relative size of the cash flows available to handle short-term commercial conflict situations, and Courtaulds with £681M can be compared with its major rivals as follows:

	£M
ICI	1524.4
Du Pont	1510
AKZO	1030
Rhone Poulenc	840
Monsanto	820

In the context of the UK market the share achieved in some areas is sufficient for large-scale production, and anyway prospective entry into EEC makes the UK a less relevant area to consider. The Group's success generally in exports in recent years demonstrates clearly the company's international competitive strength. Exports from the UK (mainly fibres and textiles) have increased as follows:

	£M
1961–62	21.6
1971–72	124.1

GOVERNMENT INFLUENCES ON MANAGEMENT THINKING

It is necessary to the main theme of the study to consider briefly at this stage the extent to which management were conscious of government attitudes and policies as a factor in taking their decisions.

In managing the Lancashire situation that consciousness was not only present but it was a dominant element in leading Courtaulds into their change of policy. The doubts and fears expressed publicly in the Chairman's statements in the 1950s and the internal analyses of the situation were formative, even if they did not lead to action; and in the early 1960s the action which was taken followed upon consultations with the senior civil servants concerned, was intended to provoke a reconsideration of government policy in the Lancashire field, and would have proved difficult to justify commercially if that reconsideration had not taken place or if those who did not believe in a viable future for the Lancashire industry had prevailed. These actions therefore provide an outstandingly interesting example of the interrelationships between government and industry. The subsequent decision to establish the new Lancashire-type weaving mills in development areas is a more simple response to government-initiated encouragement; and other investments, especially in Northern Ireland, provide further examples of responses.

Otherwise, once it was accepted that the aim generally was to secure a market share of 30 per cent or thereabouts, the verticalisation policy and the way in which it was implemented in the period under review does not appear to have been influenced consciously by government. In the latter part of the period certain individual acquisitions had to be referred to the Board of Trade for consideration under the 1965 Monopolies and Mergers Act, and the general practice was to keep the officials informed even where neither of the criteria of asset size or market share could have led to a reference to the Monopolies Commission; but, with the exception of the Calico Printers bid which led to the setting up of the Dell Committee, the required consultations were handled as a necessary routine. The Monopolies Commission inquiry which was proceeding during the latter part of the period did not influence management's views about what was necessary for the company or their actions in carrying through their verticalisation policy.

Chapter Four

THE MANAGEMENT SYSTEM

THE PROBLEMS OF DECISION AND CONTROL

In the previous chapter the emphasis has been on the strategy which was followed, the decisions through which it was implemented and the consequences for the size and shape of the Group. These were viewed against the industrial background in which Courtaulds has been operating, especially the textile industry and the other firms engaged in it.

But a firm is not just a decision-making machine, with automata to implement the decisions which emerge from rational calculation of pros and cons. It is an organism. Each firm has a life-style of its own. This is sometimes obscured in what is written about business, especially by economists whose primary interest lies in the wealth-creating and distributing processes of society, and who often find it useful to treat the firm as an entity; much as scientists regarded the atom before the work of Rutherford and others. It is also obscured by those who write about organisation as if it were independent of the individuals.

Although neither of these distortions would be accepted by those who for their various purposes are leaders in the study of business from the outside, the more simple mechanistic views of earlier generations inform some of the attitudes which are influential. No novelist has yet succeeded in the imaginative treatment of the business life in a modern large company in a way which can convey to the outsider that feel of the situation which C P Snow has (perhaps) achieved for the academic life.

This chapter, therefore, attempts to describe the management arrangements through which Courtaulds developed in the period under study, both the formal and the informal. This is necessary to an understanding both of what was required managerially to build up and sustain the structure described in the previous chapter, and of the responses to government.

THE MAIN PROBLEMS FOR MANAGEMENT

The problems which had to be dealt with did not all become apparent at the outset. Within the framework of the general textile scene, and the activities of competitors (home and overseas) and customers, the special problems peculiar to Courtaulds were as follows:

1   The speed of change. To expand from an employed capital of £234M in 1961 to £528M in 1972 is unusual, not just for the rate of change but also because Courtaulds was already a large company by UK standards at the beginning of the process.

2   The variety of new activities which were embarked on. From filament weaving and warp knitting at the beginning, the firm's textile activities alone expanded into spinning, cotton-type weaving, weft knitting, stockings, garment-making, Arachne machines and textile machine manufacture, retail and wholesale distribution. Each of these has its characteristic management needs, of which the technology—though important—is only one. The factors which it is crucial for management to handle successfully differ a great deal from one business to another and at different periods. For example in fibre manufacture there are phases during which the choice of process is predominant, in garment-making service to customers and credit control, in weaving it is design, and so on. The management skills required for one type of activity are different from those needed for others, and although there are common features to all management it is not always sufficiently appreciated that the acquired experience of each trade leads to an almost instinctive skill in handling the special problems of that trade. Management is not completely mobile between one trade and another, at least in a short period.

3   Acquisitions bring yet other problems. Even within the same trade there can be a variety of management styles, no one of which is necessarily more successful than others; nor may they be transplanted easily.

4 The vertical structure of the group brought other problems, since maximum group profit came less and less to depend on maximising profits of its constituent parts.

All of these together increased the difficulty of achieving competitive responsiveness in the downstream activities, whilst retaining control.

These problems did not all immediately become apparent in 1962. Awareness of them developed as changes were made, and the emphasis naturally switched as experience dictated. But it is convenient for an understanding of what follows thus to provide a perspective from hindsight at this point.

THE FORMAL ARRANGEMENTS

It is useful to begin by describing the formal arrangements. 'Formal' in this context means those which had been referred to the Board for approval and which applied generally throughout the Group. As compared with the earlier pre-occupation with organisation, the post-1962 period is characterised by a marked absence of concern with formal arrangements. Indeed Lord Kearton, who succeeded Dallas Bernard as Chairman on 1 November 1964, has not commented on organisation or management matters in any of the seven statements to shareholders since then; though there is a statement of faith in a speech made in Bradford in 1966 on 'Size and Efficiency in Business' in which, referring to companies with sales ranging from £300M to £700M, these comments were made:

Many of you must be thinking of the problems of organising and control of companies of the size that I am now visualising. I think there is already sufficient experience, both in the States and in the present large international corporations, to show that this problem is soluble. It does require of course a greater reliance on highly skilled professional management, but emphatically it does not require one or two superhuman beings at the top. Such companies will almost certainly organise themselves in a divisional structure. Senior managers of these divisions, together with the Board and senior staff of the parent company, will between them number several hundred. It is these men who will be carrying out the entrepreneurial function essential in the business world. Management and control can be efficiently organised by divisions having the maximum of autonomy, but still retaining the advantages of group size which stem from having access to common finance, being able to mount major research programmes, sharing common production sites and being able to co-operate in marketing and other common services where relevant.

The emphasis changes somewhat. Thus a press (*Financial Times*) report in February 1968: 'Sir Frank Kearton admits that one of his problems is how to motivate professional management to act in an entrepreneurial way.'

Throughout the period the Board itself did not change its outward characteristics to any marked degree—a body of between fifteen and eighteen men of whom two or at most three were non-executive, the remainder being full-time executives with lengthy periods of employment with the company, and with negligible shareholdings.

The table indicates that their professional background shows a marked change over the period. Meetings became less frequent—once instead of twice a month.

	1962	1972
With professional or degree qualifications		
Scientists	5	7
Engineers	1	1
Accountants	—	3
Other	2	2
Total	8	13
Without such qualifications	6	1

The important formal changes all took place in 1962. Board committees were eliminated—finance, appointments and personnel, research, customer credit, textile industry policy, subscriptions and donations and the depreciation panel. In their place two 'executives' were set up, one dealing with *Policy*, consisting of the Chairman and three senior directors; the other with *Operations*, consisting of the Chairman and seven or eight executive directors. Their functioning is described below. New financial planning arrangements were also introduced.

These financial planning arrangements were based on the existing profit centres, but they sought to bring into more coherent form the profit, capital expenditure and cash implications of their plans, looking three years ahead. As the business developed, some sixty of these profit centres were established, each with a direct responsibility to the main board, varying in size from those employing assets of £30M or more down to some with employed capital of £1M or so.

Forecasts for the coming financial year were known as budgets and were regarded as more of a commitment on managements than those for later years. The sum of these forecasts from operating units showed a pronounced tendency towards optimism or pessimism, depending on the trading conditions which prevailed at the time when the forecasts were being made. Group management, exercising its role of taking into account a wider range of factors than would be apparent to managements of operating units, found it necessary regularly to make a judgement about how much to add to or subtract from the total before forming a view about likely Group profits for the coming year.

For some years the Chairman gave shareholders an indication of likely profits which was more precise than many company chairmen would commit themselves to, and a modest pride was taken within the company at the accuracy of these indications. Future profit forecasts had played an important part in warding off the ICI bid, and the ones published at that time were received with considerable scepticism. Success in achieving forecast profits thus came to be considered as an important element in retaining credibility as a management. The record is interesting because it brings so well into focus one of the major preoccupations of senior management in this period.

Year	Forecast	Profit before tax (£M)		
		April–Sept.	Oct.–March	Full Year
1961–62	*Letter to Stockholders* (24 Jan. 1962) £17.5M	7.6	10.1	17.7
1962–63	*Letter to Stockholders* (24 Jan. 1962) £23M			
	AGM Expectations of £23M unchanged	11.1		
	Interim Profits are likely to exceed earlier forecast of £23M		12.5	23.6
1963–64	*Letter to Stockholders* (24 Jan. 1962) No forecast	15.1		
	AGM No forecast			
	Interim Expectation of second half profits being similar to first half		18.2	33.3
1964–65	*Letter to Stockholders* (24 Jan. 1962) £28.5M	17.3		
	AGM No forecast			
	Interim Expectation of second half profit being slightly less than first half		19.1	36.4
1965–66	*Letter to Stockholders* (24 Jan. 1962) No forecast	17.1		
	AGM No forecast			
	Interim Second half similar to first half		19.9	37.0
1966–67	*AGM* No forecast	16.1		
	Interim (if UK conditions become more normal) Second half profits will be similar to first half		16.1	32.2
1967–68	*AGM* (a) First half will be down by £2 to £3M			
	(b) ... at best a static year for profits	13.1		
	Interim Indications are that second half profits will not improve on first half as was hoped		22.7	35.8
1968–69	*AGM* (a) First half will exceed £17M, might exceed £18M			
	(b) Full year of over £40M	21.1		
	(c) Target for early seventies £50M			
	Interim Not less than £45M for full year		29.8	50.9
1969–70	*AGM* Some profit growth, albeit on a modest scale for the full year (on £50.9M)	23.4		
	Interim Second half should be similar to second half of last year		28.7	52.1
1970–71	*AGM* (a) First half will be down by roughly 25% (=down to £17.55M)	17.6		
	(b) Second half 'will progressively improve'			
	Interim Should be about £40M		24.1	41.7
1971–72	*AGM* (a) First half will be down on 1970–71	16.2		
	(b) Second half should see recovery from the setbacks		29.3	45.5

The budget profits for each month compared with actual gave a quick indication of where things might be going wrong and by insisting on the actual figure within a few days after the end of the month, this information was available for timely action.

In the formal arrangements, the operating managements each responsible for a profit centre play the key role. The appropriate grouping of the newly acquired activities was actively debated. For example, there were many who advocated a new division to embrace the garment activities, seeing this as the best way to identify management responsibility and to provide machinery for planning and control, especially in commercial matters. But these views were consistently opposed by the Chairman, despite his public acceptance in the 1966 Bradford speech of the need for a divisional structure. His emphasis was much more on finding managers who could demonstrate success and then enlarging their responsibilities; and this view prevailed, so that those who look for a divisional pattern bringing activities into some coherent structure will not find it.

The central or service staffs have responsibilities which include finance and accounting, research, commercial, employee relations, legal, government, etc. In January 1963 the former central engineering staff was reorganised into a separate company and required to operate at a profit, though a substantial part of its turnover (never less than 50 per cent) was with Group companies and for much of its work there would be no practicable alternative source of supply. Otherwise the central staffs were regarded either as providing services for which the operating divisions would negotiate an appropriate fee, or as exercising a control or corporate function such as accounting. Managements of operating units could expect to receive the attentions of these central control departments whatever their wishes in the matter and were therefore not expected to carry any share of their costs. The annual bargaining between units and service departments sometimes becomes absurdly prolonged and time-consuming, and there is an unrealistic element in that units may not go elsewhere for services such as research. Generally those managements with least confidence in their ability to cope with their primary tasks appear to be the most preoccupied with interdepartmental wrangling. But the system is on balance believed to help towards efficiency and of course provides a cross-check on some aspects of unit management's activities.

THE TOP MANAGEMENT GROUP

But all this is peripheral to the main central planning and control functions with which the exiguous formal organisation arrangements alone are quite insufficient to cope. These functions are carried out by the Chairman and the executive directors acting as individuals, though with the authority of the Board and its Operations Executive. The system places a load on individual executive directors. These, with exceptions to be mentioned, each take responsibility for a group of profit centres; the spread between the directors depends on who the individuals are, where the problem situations are seen to be, and the changing conceptions of the interrelationships between profit centres in the Group context. These executive directors are thus in effect senior general managers.

The exceptions are the Chairman, the two deputy chairmen (one covering commercial, the other administrative matters) and the finance director. These four have a more complete view of what the Group is about than others, and of these the Chairman, as chief executive and the only one with no limitations as to role, is clearly the key figure.

In any large company only a few individuals have this complete view of what is going on, and some generalisations about how businessmen think or act are misleading because they reflect what has been said by those who, even sometimes in senior positions, are protected by their roles from a full realisation of what is afoot. They do not always appreciate the risks which attend the decisions and actions of the few senior managers.

And the same consideration explains the preoccupation with profitability which sometimes appears exaggerated and even inhuman both to well-disposed observers and to managers in less exposed jobs. But, being protected by their roles, some of these can easily act in ways inimical to the Group interest—the sales executive with his preoccupation with volume, the engineer seeking to build monuments to his professional skill, those in all places who would like a quiet life, and so on. The pressure towards profitability supplies a common logic to which these diverse and sometimes conflicting personal goals can be made hopefully to conform.

It is impossible to consider the development of Courtaulds within the period except in the light of the extraordinary achievement of one man. This is no place to examine the characteristics and influences which were responsible for the combination in one man of the qualities which were crucial. For the present purpose it is sufficient to recognise that those qualities existed, and that the absence of formal organisation arrangements permitted their exercise with fewer of the restraints than would be conceivable to outsiders with pre-conceived ideas about business management.

In formulating plans, the techniques were based on a capacity to absorb the information available from a host of sources inside and outside the company, relating to economic trends, technology, market developments and the industrial structure; and then to integrate this almost intuitively into precise proposals to acquire this or that company, or to build a factory for a particular product, or to re-equip an existing group of factories. This capacity for innovation in the realm of ideas was of course particularly displayed at an early stage in formulating the Northern Plan described in the previous chapter. The internal information on which these judgements were formed included research reports, economic studies relating to the textile industry and reports from specialists visiting factories which might be acquired.

Generally no other single individual would have had access to the full range of information, or indeed would have the capacity to absorb it, quite apart from forming practical conclusions for action from it. So that the shared discussion of plans usually followed a process of private study and thought which, combined with unusual skill in debate and speed of positive reaction to newly-raised doubts, usually shortened the time needed for debate. All others, fully stretched in their respective specialist roles, were so much less prepared to be capable of expressing a point of view which carried conviction. The two or three exceptions where the doubts and hesitations were sufficiently generally held to make it inopportune to force through a decision serve only to emphasise the more usual acquiescence. This is not to say that all decisions were always right, but effective management action can so often make a success of decisions which have been taken, irrespective of that intellectual balancing of pros and cons which is so much more interesting to those who study decision-taking from outside and looms so large in some discussions of the subject.

Advisers play a part in decision-taking and the dividing line between research and action is not always clear-cut. The information which is supplied is intended to influence action and the advisers who prepare it sometimes have strong personal views which can affect the information they choose to emphasise. In a continually developing process, such as that described in the previous chapter, it is to be expected that the sheer interest of the job will lead some advisers—especially the more able—to form strong views of their own; and they must then make the transition to being managers. Otherwise the research teams can become power centres without responsibility and diminish the effectiveness (for good or ill) of those who are responsible.

This is no more than a special case of the way in which all individuals change in response to their experiences. The top management group were influenced by the events of the 1950s described in the first chapter; these events provided the inheritance with which they had to deal in the 1960s, and thus influenced the way they behaved.

INFORMATION FOR CONTROL

Control means information about what is happening and corrective action if that is needed—with maximum group profitability as the touchstone by which all proposals and actions must be judged.

The period which is relevant for this purpose depends on

the nature of the activity being considered. In the period under study and in the Courtaulds situation a time-horizon of ten years is about the maximum which can ever be realistically considered even when dealing with the most fundamental strategic issues. The one exception relates to the recruitment and training of individuals with an eye to a lifetime career, but here again there is only a limited degree to which it is worthwhile to attempt precisely to plan the skills an individual will need or the job changes he and the company will find useful.

The maximum ten-year time-horizon relates closely to the period which senior executives spend at the peak of their careers; the average executive director has a period of about twelve years in that position and this has some influence on the length of time he has in mind in making plans, quite apart from the commercial uncertainties which make longer-term plans a waste of effort. And for most management purposes a much shorter time-horizon is appropriate.

The information needed for control is, as indicated above, only partly provided through the formal reporting machinery established in 1962. This was later supplemented, especially during the intense credit restraint when customers were only too anxious to use suppliers as bankers, by regular systematic analyses of debtors and overdue payments, and by similar reviews of stocks. But throughout the period the informal information arrangements initiated by individual executive directors have been the more important for action, and of these the Chairman's arrangements have been the most extensive and most effective. They include personal reports from managers at all levels (of which the relevant executive director usually ensures that he sees a copy), telephone calls to that individual at whatever level in the hierarchy who is most likely to have the needed information, and a few personal staff, roving ambassadors.

This flow of rapidly assimilated detailed information is the basis for corrective action. A piecemeal approach to implementing investment decisions (where this is possible) permits the adverse effects of some wrong decisions to be minimised.

THE OPERATIONS AND POLICY EXECUTIVES

In this situation the Operations Executive, meeting twice a month, serves two functions. It sets a formal seal upon plans and management changes which have been thoroughly debated beforehand by some of those present. This does not mean that it automatically rubberstamps proposals, but rather that proposals may sometimes be referred back for further consideration. It also provides a forum for identifying the attitudes and actions to be adopted in dealing with those aspects of operations which are of high priority, followed by any needed indoctrination. Thus in the cash shortage of 1970 and 1971 debtors generally sought to gain extended credit from suppliers, and it became important to monitor the effectiveness of what individual managements were doing. Later, with rapidly rising costs, it became important to put the emphasis on increasing selling prices.

This function of identifying the area in which management action is needed and exerting pressure to achieve it, is of course quite inconsistent with the principles of delegation as they are widely understood and practised. But repeated failures enforce the lesson that this is a key function of top management, that good middle management is not all so easily found, and that only an occasional failure can be dealt with by replacement with somebody better. But failures are not voluntarily brought to the light of day, and to discover them and then to seek to train and educate the available talent is a major preoccupation. This aspect of the Operations Executive's role is stressed because it runs counter to so much accepted doctrine; it does nevertheless represent an important element in getting a feel of the internal running of the business.

The Policy Executive plays a more limited role. It deals with the preliminary discussion of administrative matters which are particularly confidential, such as new board appointments. It is also the forum for discussing long-range strategic plans, though not exclusively, for informal discussion amongst individual executive directors is at least as important.

INDIVIDUAL MANAGERS AND A MANAGEMENT STYLE

The working arrangements can best be described by selecting a few key areas of management for more detailed discussion. Strategic planning has already been mentioned and this is perhaps the most crucial for the theme of the present study.

The process by which new products pass through the various phases of research, technical development, project planning, equipment selection, project implementation, running-in of new plants and commercial exploitation, is probably less relevant to the theme of this study, important though it is to the successful running of the business. More germane to the theme, perhaps, is the selection, training and developing of managers, because the possibilities and limitations in this respect have an important bearing on what it is feasible to expect by way of behaviour; and linked with this are the methods and limitations of the techniques for monitoring and control of the policies which have been decided.

The senior managers with whom alone this study need be concerned are those earning £6000 a year or more, of whom in 1972 there are about 240 employed in the UK. (Throughout this study the overseas activities of the Group, representing about 20 per cent of the whole, whatever test is used, are of only incidental interest.) Of these thirty-nine were paid at an annual rate of £10 000 or above on 31 March 1972 (excluding directors). Although they include senior professional staff, the greater number are in general management, some with a commercial or production bias in larger units.

But the variety of activities in which the Group is engaged calls more and more for an all-round ability to handle a business as a self-contained entity, subject to the requirements which arise from their forming part of a larger group. In the present context, for example, the needs of the vertical pattern are the most important. 'Entrepreneurs capable of acting in the Group interest' is an apt description.

Such individuals come from two main sources: those recruited into the Courtaulds/Celanese business with more than ten years' service; and those who have gained their experience in the more recently acquired companies. Few of those in senior positions have joined at a mature age after a business career elsewhere.

This also reflects the fact that each company has its own style, including ways of behaving which minimise the need for formal communication and thus achieving a speed of response which is more difficult for organisations which require bureaucratic procedures because of the nature of their roles. The process of acquiring that knowledge of 'how things are done here' is gradual; when learnt, the knowledge represents a substantial hidden asset possessed by those who have been successfully trained within the organisation—and places the mature newcomer at a severe disadvantage. The management style which is thus established needs to be appropriate to the situation.

A former chairman in one of his memoranda referred approvingly to the 'gentleman's club atmosphere' which had prevailed in Courtaulds' boardroom for many years, and this carried implications about the atmosphere which prevailed in other parts of the organisation. 'The company can afford it' was a common enough comment. Such a style would have been incompatible with changes at the speed and on the scale which were necessary later, or with the competitive situations in which these changes were occurring. A major effort was needed to remove traces of the old style and to engender a new one more suitable to the needs. This could only stem from the top. How was it done?

Some aspects have been mentioned—getting people to accept that information will be sought from whoever might have it without respect for hierarchy, breaking down entrenched ideas about what effective delegation means. Other techniques have been a willingness to exhort and explain face-to-face, the use of all of the skills of cajoling, bullying, rewarding and chastising (sometimes at the same time), eschewing meetings, keeping office doors open and encouraging rapid and frequent informal consultation. All these add up to a new style which some managers attempt to copy with varying degrees of success. Pomp and circumstance and a preoccupation with hierarchy seem generally to be associated with a lack of flexibility and confidence. Those who thrive are the more able; those who suffer are the ones who need more visible supports to their power and authority, because they lack the inner resources necessary to cope with such a variety of changing situations.

There is a bigger element of luck in success than the successful are usually prepared to admit. Success in one area of business is no guide to the likelihood of success in a different area; and even in the same area a run of success appears sometimes to engender a euphoria which inhibits the very qualities needed to cope with any deterioration which often follows a success period, at least for a while. All of this means that there is no permanent cadre of proven managers capable of dealing with any situation. Success in management is painfully achieved through patient fostering and renewal. So there is no proven route, and management development schemes which purport to identify the successful performers of the future can badly mislead both the individuals and senior management. The qualities of an individual's immediate seniors in the early years of a career appear to be the most important single factor in success, and the good teacher shows an interest in the young and the patience to find the time for it.

In the rapid development of the post-1962 period, the most abundant source of talent for management training proved to be the research division. This is a testimony to the work of those who built up the research team in the 1950s from its negligible beginnings in the immediate post-war years, and to the working methods which required the scientists who had developed new processes or improvements of existing ones to spend time in the factories attending to the practical application of their laboratory results. With a research department of about 300 graduates and an annual recruitment of about sixty, about forty a year move out of research into management jobs or jobs with a management potential; this has a further advantage of constantly replenishing the pool of talent in the research team.

In this respect Courtaulds is more successful than those organisations in which the research team is confined to its primary task. A high proportion of those now in senior posts first joined the company as research workers. This means that there is a special training problem because those who have succeeded in research feel more at ease with production and technical matters, and sometimes give too little attention to their financial and commercial problems.

Senior management is evidently engaged in a training job which is never finished, and the best managers are those who are prepared to adjust to the lessons to be learned from their mistakes. So the control and monitoring activities described above find their chief usefulness in contributing to this process. Black and white distinctions between good and bad management are seldom possible. Every failure is in part a reflection on those who appointed and were responsible for supervising. The ultimate sanction of dismissal is seldom exercised before there has been a series of failures, followed by an attempt to discover what can be achieved by a transfer to some new activity requiring a different balance of qualities.

The techniques for monitoring and control thus result in action which is much more concerned with the long-term development of a management team than would sometimes appear to the individuals themselves. They are conscious of the checks and probings to which their actions are being subjected, and to the immediate critical and sometimes explosive responses to their personal shortcomings. The idea that managers are left alone to do their jobs and are then judged by results may possibly be applicable in organisations which are developing steadily, and where there has been time to build up a consensus as to the danger situations which can arise and the appropriate responses to them; but it has little validity in the series of situations which arise in a company with such a disparity of activities forming one whole, as Courtaulds. It follows that since only a few senior people at the top have the full information about the changing situation, a major part of their effort must be devoted to those monitoring and control activities of finding out what is happening, intervening, cajoling, preaching and bullying, sometimes deliberately creating stress situations without which many otherwise able people cannot be induced to modify their behaviour. And mingling this with more encouraging actions—praise, more public recognition of success, suitable material rewards in great variety and with varying mixes at the level of seniority now being considered.

In time perhaps some of this activity can become codified into patterns of behaviour and into teachable techniques, and indeed the strain on the few individuals concerned is such that this must be done eventually for the pioneering effort cannot be sustained indefinitely. Meanwhile, however, the accomplishment of the changes described in the preceding chapter sometimes felt like a labour of Sisyphus.

The conscious direction to the Group's strategy in this period was to build up a vertical structure from fibre-making to fibre-using, but with external as well as internal sales at every stage. This resulted in a balance of activities quite different from that of any other fibre or textile company in the world.

The special management problems which followed from this ought in principle to have been dealt with by devising suitable transfer pricing arrangements. Individual unit managements seeking to maximise the profits of their units, bargaining with supplying units and free to buy from competitors, and bargaining with customer units equally free to buy from competitors, would together fail to maximise Group profits. Profits in the difficult years 1970 and 1971, though inadequate, compared favourably with those of all other fibre producers in the UK, Europe and North America and this is a consequence of the successful exploitation of the vertical structure. Despite excess fibre capacity throughout the industry, and a degree of price competition incompatible with long-term viability, Courtaulds managed to operate at higher capacity levels and to be more selective than others in its pricing policies. But this required firm direction from central management to override what appeared at times to be the short-term interest of some unit managements.

The Group's nylon activities provide a good example of the management approaches which are needed. Nylon is one of the fibres whose production has been most over-expanded and therefore was most unprofitable in the low activity years of 1970 and 1971. The launching of Courtaulds' nylon project in 1964 has been described in the previous chapter. It was crucial to getting established at this late stage that the Group's own substantial and expanding users of nylon should switch to the new product. The warp knitting division was one of these. But initially, as a new and inexperienced producer, the nylon division was unable to meet competitive quality standards. Independent warp knitters would have had no incentive to persist, but since the Group's needs were made manifest, the troublesome two years which would have made it impossible for a new independent producer to survive were overcome. The expanded stocking activities, also large users of nylon, bought at prices which were higher than those offered by outside suppliers, but have resisted the pressures to reduce their selling prices to the extent that drove some of their competitors into making losses, and this concerted commercial strategy achieved a relative success in these two difficult years.

To convey some sense of the intellectual and emotional atmosphere in which these events occurred is essential because it provides that element without which nothing would happen —that which Keynes once described as 'animal spirits.' As in all human situations the possible perspectives are almost without limit in a Group employing 150 000 people each with relatives upon whom the Group's activities make an impact, and customers, suppliers, public officials, trade union officials and others. Within the company a broad distinction can be made between the few who knew a lot of the total picture and were aware of what was at stake and the risks being run, and the many—including some in senior positions—protected by their roles from the full realisation of what was afoot. The contrast is best brought out by the comment of the junior manager at the fifty-year award ceremony, who opened his speech by stressing the feeling of having been protected for fifty years by the great organisation for which he had worked, and on the other side, the reaction of one of the deputy chairmen that at no time in his career had he ever felt any security.

SOME FORMATIVE PRESSURES AND OPPORTUNITIES

For the present purpose the only valid perspective would be that of the individual who was most responsible for the strategy and the management of carrying it out, for the company would not have developed in anything like the way it did in this period if that individual had not made it happen. Failing that, a close observer (and occasional participant—which might introduce its own bias) of the scene throughout the period would identify a few key strands. No one of these could be left out of account without a serious loss of understanding of the processes which were going on, but it is appropriate to leave aside any assessment of whatever in inheritance or upbringing or experience might have formed the characters in this scene and to concentrate only on those manifestations of these deeper roots which appeared in the business activity. In seeking to capture the feel of the situations which together have produced the present company, six key emotional and intellectual strands can be identified.

SOME PRINCIPAL MOTIVATING FORCES

Survival

First in importance has been the feeling that the continued separate existence of the company has been at risk. Following the ICI offer and its partial failure, a few individuals in Courtaulds had staked their personal reputations, not just on achieving the particular profit forecasts which had been publicised, but also on achieving a continued independent existence for Courtaulds; or if that proved impossible, on making sure that the terms for any merger were as favourable as possible. This sprang not so much from any deepfelt sense of obligation to Courtaulds' shareholders, but more from a personal pride, of which the shareholders' interest became a convenient symbol.

The feeling that the company was engaged in a struggle to survive persisted beyond the time during which it was necessary to satisfy the expectations aroused during the ICI affair. Indeed, there emerged a recognition that a merger with ICI might well have been a sensible policy—certainly a more congenial way of life for the Courtaulds men concerned—if only the matter had been differently handled on both sides. As the situation developed, the persistent sense of being at risk derived much more from the actions of, or threats from, other external pressures.

Fibre competition

Those pressures exerted by competitive fibre producers were the most direct and all-pervasive. A few of the more important ones can be mentioned to give some idea of their scope. In the domestic market there was intense competition from European producers of viscose rayon staple, especially from those in Scandinavia and Austria (the arrangements with whom provided such a feature of the Monopolies Commission inquiry). In the UK acetate fibre market, Celanese had a dominant position but this was under constant attack from the small producer Lansil. This was especially so after it was bought by Monsanto, the US chemical and fibre concern which had already established nylon and acrylic fibre plants in the UK taking advantage especially of the financial help offered in Northern Ireland. The acquisition by ICI of one of the major acetate yarn users was followed by a further erosion of the Courtaulds/Celanese position in the domestic market.

In Europe the use of acetate had not been developed to the same extent as in North America or the UK, and British Celanese has thus been able to build up a substantial business either by selling yarns or by collaborating with the Courtaulds woven and warp knit fabric producers. The competition initially was with the European acetate producers, and with the producers in Europe of the viscose yarns which acetate could hope to displace, but the more aggressive entry of American Celanese into the market with a local plant in Luxembourg intensified these pressures.

In the UK, British Celanese had also established itself as the major supplier of tow for the manufacture of cigarette tips, but this position was attacked through a joint project between the biggest UK buyer of tow and Tennessee Eastman, the major USA producer, again taking full advantage of development area facilities and local borrowing possibilities. (Thus a £6M project required a cash investment of only £600 000 from the two parties with the main commercial interest in it). In this case the UK capacity was already adequate, and the new plant is still (end 1971) operating at a loss. The Celanese capacity for cigarette tow has been diverted to produce mainly for export markets where profit margins are less satisfactory. It must be an open question whether this type of competition leads to the most efficient use of UK resources.

In the UK acrylic market, the competition has come in part from Monsanto (already mentioned, page 88) and in part from Du Pont, also operating in Northern Ireland with substantial financial aid. In the period before local production began, the UK market was supplied by importation and in the summer of 1967 a price reduction of 20 per cent was provoked by them at a time when the volume of their sales was too small for this to be an important matter. For Courtaulds, however, this move meant a reduction in profits at the rate of £3M a year. The expansion of the market and Courtaulds' plans for achieving a substantial share of it would have required such a price reduction at some stage; but the timing enforced by competition was most inconvenient.

At this stage in the development of the acrylic fibres the most important route for their use was through the worsted spinning system, and CPB was and remains a major customer in this area, expanding by internal growth and by acquiring other worsted spinners. However the scale of the expansion which was foreseen and the need for some diversity of marketing outlets led Courtaulds to decide on a massive expansion (until then their stake in worsted spinning had been relatively small), building a new plant at Spennymoor in Co Durham.

Import competition
In addition to these pressures from other fibre suppliers there was the continuing competition from imports of fabrics and garments, especially those from low-wage cost countries; of which the duty-free imports under the Ottawa agreements were, of course, particularly troublesome. This subject is dealt with in the following chapter, but it must be mentioned here as one part of the general framework of competitive pressures which made the period feel like a continuing struggle for survival.

Industry fragmentation

The concentration of retail buying power into fewer large groups was also proceeding. Some 40 per cent of all textiles are now bought by fifteen or so large groups.

The fragmentation of the intermediate processes of converting fibres into finished textile products creates yet other competitive pressures. In the Lancashire section of the industry this will be described further in Chapter 5, but in other areas the number of manufacturing firms is also excessive in relation to the concentration of retail buying power. This combination of pressures created a strong feeling of being in a hostile world and, since the pressures arose in an intense form at differing times, there was a sense of conducting the struggle for survival on a number of fronts.

Risk-taking

All this activity in dealing with the external threats was accompanied by a more positive constructive action to carry through the programme described in Chapter 3. Here the management was dealing with situations about which there could be a modest confidence, given good management and some good luck. But they were all risk situations and the second main strand in this account of how it felt at the time consists in this consciousness, that each decision is to some extent a gamble which, however well handled, might fail.

This consciousness was particularly acute in 1964 when it was decided, having sold the BNS share to ICI, to go ahead with an independent nylon project. It was known to be late in the day—for nylon had been a commercial success from about 1950 onwards; and it was on the basis of no more than the small pilot plant which had been acquired with Celanese in 1957, since Courtaulds' research and technical personnel had been allowed no access to what BNS were doing. So acute was this feeling that big issues were at stake that, although there had been no dissension in the discussions which preceded the formal decision, it was one of the three or so occasions during the period on which each member of the Board individually identified himself with the decision. This was no decision by acquiescence.

A similar consciousness attended the decision later in 1964 to acquire LCC and FSD at a cost of £36M. There had been no change in government policy, and it would have been unrealistic against the background of all that had occurred to have sought any assurances about a change in government policy. It could only be hoped that vigorous action to demonstrate the possibility of a viable industry in Lancashire would bring forth the necessary responses.

But the initial acquisitions were only the first step. To match international levels of productivity in spinning, a massive investment in new equipment would clearly be necessary. And something would have to be done about the subsequent weaving process for it was obvious that the existing industry, or large parts of it, could not survive; thus there was no certainty of there being any domestic customers for a modernised spinning industry. Subsequently the decision was taken to deal with this situation by establishing new weaving mills in development areas, using modern and in some instances unproven equipment.

These examples of the risks which had to be taken will convey an additional dimension to the atmosphere which prevailed. But each risk, though substantial, was nicely calculated, and the commitments wherever possible were entered upon in a step-by-step fashion so that the gamble at each stage was minimised until further information had come to light to enable the next steps to be planned. It was also recognised that with so many new developments under way a failure in one area, although to be avoided at whatever expense of management effort was necessary, if unavoidable would not cripple the business. There was a consciousness that management was handling a portfolio of risk situations and that there was some balancing of the risks.

This was brought clearly into perspective in the discussions which preceded the decision to join one of the consortia engaged in exploring for gas in the North Sea. The initial commitment was to invest £500 000, which was modest in the context of Courtaulds' cash resources. But those who opposed the investment did so not because it was a gamble, but because if it succeeded it would lead to increasingly large further calls for cash until the sums at stake would be crippling in the event of failure. And with success the sums required did indeed escalate in a way which led Courtaulds to limit their commitment, until the investment was finally sold (at a handsome profit).

Tension
The final strand in the emotional/intellectual history of the period consists in the sheer excitement of battle. Some of the conflict situations have been referred to in discussing the competitive pressures. Others arose in dealing with proposed acquisitions where there was opposition from the managements, or a competitive bid or the threat of one. These situations have been described sufficiently often for any detailed account to be unnecessary, but the heightened awareness and the tenseness which comes of having an external enemy is a stimulant.

The tensions of internal disagreement are of quite a different quality. They are equally powerful, however, and in the long run more important because they affect personal relationships and colour other activities. It is therefore necessary to limit the number of occasions on which disagreements are pushed to the point of conflict. The occasions must relate to issues of major importance on which the individuals concerned are prepared if necessary to resign, which means that such occasions tend to have strong emotional overtones and cannot be ignored in any account of 'how it feels'.

But whereas these are necessarily rare (if they became frequent there would have to be some changes in the personalities running the business), the day-to-day management described earlier in this chapter provides the continuing emotional content of the business life. The frustrations arise from the inability or unwillingness of others to act in ways which appear only too obvious to those who carry the responsibility and also from accepting that—with occasional exceptions—the existing talent is the best available and as a result of sustained effort perhaps better in some respects than that of the competitors. The limitations of working through direct instructions soon became obvious. So various are the situations that a lot has to be left to the man on the spot; and yet occasionally he has to be overruled. Unless this is done in unequivocal terms, he will interpret the situation in his own way and perhaps even evade instructions to suit his conception of the need.

The few at the centre can so easily become considered like the Greek gods, creatures with human failings, capricious in their interventions—but dangerous because they have real power if they choose to direct their attention. The problem is often glibly described as one of communication, but it is more fundamental than that. Handling people in an organism like Courtaulds which has changed so quickly and in so many ways is a strain, because it is never-ending. Those concerned in the process sometimes envy the barrister who deals with one brief and then passes to the next, who has no need to suffer fools gladly because his work is entirely with his intellectual peers. Although this may be an illusion, as outsiders' judgements of other people's lives so often are, it may help by contrast to evoke the dominant feeling of those engaged in translating a business plan into action.

Part Two

COURTAULDS AND THE GOVERNMENT

Chapter Five

GOVERNMENT AND THE TEXTILE INDUSTRY

BACKGROUND

The description in Chapter 2 of the environment with which the Courtaulds management were conscious of having to deal in the post-1962 years identified the Lancashire problem as the focal point for action by the company, and for interaction between the company and the government. The two preceding chapters have concentrated upon the course of action pursued by the company. However, government policy towards the textile industry necessarily extended well beyond its concern with the Lancashire situation. There were, indeed, two aspects to policy: industry structure, and protection against imports.

Government concern with structure has come about from two directions. First, it has come from attempts to deal with the Lancashire industry problems (to be described in this chapter). And secondly it derived from a more general pre-occupation with the possible disadvantages to the public interest if individual companies secure a substantial share of the market. This involved the substantial Monopolies Commission inquiry and the various investigations by the former National Board for Prices and Incomes. These are described in the next chapter.

But attitudes deriving from the monopolies legislation also influenced the debate about the structure of the textile industry, and in reading this chapter it must be borne in mind that a one-third share of a market is sufficient to bring an activity within the scope of the legislation. In most sectors of the textile industry, other than manmade fibre production, a market share of this size represented (in the period under study) such

D

an advance from the fragmentation which otherwise prevailed that nobody found it worthwhile arguing whether the test was relevant to long-term viability. No doubt this issue of market share will become less important in the present decade, especially in the context of membership of the European Common Market. In the present chapter, however, the significance of market shares in relation to the public interest is important in understanding the degree and kind of attention the industry attracted from the government.

TRADE POLICY

From an industrial point of view, it can be asserted that where —as in textiles—government-influenced purchases are relatively unimportant, the levels of and methods employed for the protection of domestic industry against foreign imports provide the most important area for industry–government interaction. Although the subject has a long history, this is not necessary to resurrect until, as in Lancashire, the issue becomes politically sensitive. But throughout the period there was, quite apart from the Lancashire problem, a continuing and important dialogue on the subject of protection.

For the developed countries, the textile industry offers under modern conditions as good a way of using resources as other types of manufacturing industry; the glamour industries of ten years ago now look less glamorous. But there is a conflict between the desire of the developed countries to maintain employment in textiles, and the urge of less developed countries to seek growth by establishing export-oriented textile industries. With labour as a factor of diminishing importance, cost comparisons do not point clearly in either direction. Most governments give substantial help. In developed countries this takes the form of restrictions on imports (USA, Japan, France, Italy), export subsidies (Austria) or special offers of investment assistance (Japan, Italy).

The UK market has been less protected than that of other developed countries—in part because of the consequences of the bargain with Commonwealth countries under the Ottawa agreements of 1932, which among other things provided that cotton textiles from the Commonwealth had (until 1972) duty-free access, in part because UK governments have been at times more dedicated than others to the pursuit of greater freedom in international trade.

Imports in one form or another (fibres, fabrics, or garments) have now captured more than 50 per cent of the UK domestic market. There has been a continuing conflict between the interests of employees in the UK industry and the consequences of aiming at a liberal world trading régime. As a great exporter the UK stood to gain more than she lost from such a policy. It was incidental that in textiles the benefit happened to go chiefly to developing countries.

In the 1960–70 decade this basic conflict influenced the way in which a number of issues were dealt with. The more important were as follows:

1 The UK Commercial Treaty with Japan, under which the textile and clothing industry was by and large regarded as 'sensitive' and useful important restraint levels established.
2 The GATT Long Term Arrangement of October 1962 which major developed countries invoked to regulate their imports of cotton textiles.
3 The EFTA agreements which gave more easy access to the UK market—in a way which particularly affected Courtaulds—to fibre producers in Austria, Finland and Norway whose governments (because indigenous raw materials were being exploited) had powerful reasons to support those producers in various ways.
4 The UNCTAD proposals where the UK government, unlike others, specifically excluded textiles from the scope of any negotiations on tariff preferences to increase trade with the less developed countries.
5 The 'Kennedy Round' negotiations to reduce tariff levels multilaterally.
6 The UK decision to impose tariffs on Commonwealth cotton textiles, and later also simultaneously to maintain the previous quota system; and
7 Repercussions from the increased protection of the US textile industry.

The abortive 1961–62 negotiations with EEC and the detailed negotiations under the 1971 agreement for entry into EEC have so far provided no firm arrangements affecting textiles.

In all these matters ambivalent attitudes towards the UK textile industry were apparent, and they led to the inconsistent fostering or weakening of the industry or segments of it. More generally they have perpetuated the atmosphere of uncertainty which is inimical to long-term planning and the taking of long-term industrial commitments.

In 1957 an informal group of individuals from all sectors of the textile industry—the Derby Group—was set up to deal with the first negotiations for a Free Trade Area involving all Europe. This has been a most successful two-way channel for the whole industry in dealing with government on the detailed issues. Major policy would always be discussed at or near Permanent Secretary level by those immediately concerned; but the success of the Derby Group has been due to its wide coverage, its informality and flexibility. It provides a forum where all sectors of the multi-fibre, multi-process UK textile industry (including clothing) can thrash out a common policy opposite government. A remarkable degree of common interest has been established; separate sectional representations are of course open to all members particularly where (in what has proved over the years to be a relatively small area) there is a genuine difference of opinion. It provides a focal point for consultation by Whitehall and has been active on all international trade questions including GATT tariff rounds, the UNCTAD preference scheme, USA trade policy, Anglo-Japanese and other bilateral trade negotiations, EFTA questions of origin, drawback, etc, and UK adherence to the enlarged European Community of Nine.

The industry's more formal arrangements for dealing with government have consisted in sectional bodies to represent the interests of the traditionally separate parts of the industry— wool, Lancashire, hosiery and so on—and in organisations of wider scope, though none (so far) embracing all the interests of the industry.

The remainder of this chapter describes three examples of

the interaction between government and the textile industry. The first was the most significant both for the industry and in the context of this study. It is therefore dealt with at greater length.

THE TEXTILE COUNCIL REPORT OF 1969

Some early history
The Textile Council study, which led to the writing of the Report, was initiated in 1966 by a letter from Sir Richard Powell, then Permanent Secretary at the Board of Trade. It was seen as one more step in the series of measures to deal with the Lancashire section of the textile industry.

This part of the industry, though accounting at that time for no more than about 16 per cent of the total net output, had become the object of particular attention because, first, the economic pressures described in Chapter 2 had impinged upon it with more force than on other parts of the industry; and secondly Lancashire included a number of marginal constituencies, so that its troubles engaged the interest of politicians especially at times when the political balance was unstable.

The separate identity of the Lancashire section of the industry derived from the time when it had been a major exporter and from the structure which had been appropriate to that role. Traditional distinctions between one section of the industry and another went deep. The merchant converters had a powerful influence. The cycle of successively good and bad periods of trade was widely believed to be a consequence of the industry's peculiar structure.

In 1930, the Clynes Committee on the Cotton Industry blamed the marketing system for the industry losing its export trade to Far Eastern Commonwealth production of coarse standard cotton piecegoods, and recommended changes in structure and organisation in spinning and weaving so that these sectors would be better equipped to formulate clear production policies and would better balance the finishing and merchanting sectors in which substantial combination had already occurred. In the poor trading conditions of the time, however, the recommendations were not palatable to the industry. Instead, it chose to fall back on a policy of work-sharing which put a premium on inefficiency and had a discouraging effect on those firms which had modern equipment and relatively high fixed costs and capital charges, whose profit margins disappeared as their output fell.

In 1944 the Platt Mission to the USA recommended re-equipment for the longer term and made interim suggestions for increasing productivity, including greater standardisation of output. In 1946 a Board of Trade Working Party compared the findings of the Platt Mission with current productivity levels in the UK, and found that the level of standardisation achieved under wartime conditions gave financial returns per loom up to three times better (in spite of price control) than had been calculated on the basis of pre-war experience. However, both the ordering practices of merchants and a complex wage structure (under which operatives could earn more per hour on fancy than on plain cloths) acted against more economic patterns of output. The large quantities of usable equipment lying idle, as well as the shortage of labour, combined with a boom situation to minimise any incentives felt by firms to re-equip and reorganise. The balance of trade worsened after the slump of 1951 as competition increased from the largely re-equipped textile industries in Europe, as well as from the lower-cost Commonwealth producers and from Japan. Labour and union opposition to change continued, as well as the survival in business of a large number of marginal firms aided by the price-fixing arrangements of spinners and finishers. Imports increased rapidly from 1954 to 1958.

In 1957 the shadow President of the Board of Trade, Harold Wilson, prepared a memorandum at the request of the United Textile Factory Workers Association advocating a number of measures. These included tax incentives to encourage investment, government-provided buildings and machinery on favourable terms, an Imports Commission to control imports of cotton yarns and piecegoods 'if the problem of Indian imports cannot be settled by private negotiations,' and a Reorganisation Commission to draw up schemes for amalgamation and to encourage appropriate vertical groupings. These ideas were endorsed and enlarged upon by George Brown in July 1963 with particular emphasis on regulating imports.

First signs of government action

In 1958 Harold Macmillan, then Prime Minister, gave an assurance that the government would consider sympathetically any plans put forward by the industry which involved 'a measure of direct help.' But the White Paper of May 1959 (Cmd. 744) was explicit that duty-free import of cotton goods from the Commonwealth was one aspect of the Imperial Preference system which we could not dismantle if we wished at the same time to keep those advantages which Commonwealth countries gave in their markets. It also stated that 'we are living at a time when the West must pursue liberal economic policies towards the younger countries of the emerging continents if they are to be convinced that our way of life is the best pattern for themselves.' This expressed an attitude which has consistently influenced discussion of the industry's problems. It springs in part from feelings of guilt about the supposed iniquities of British colonialism in its heyday and, whatever may be the historical evidence to justify or gainsay, it leads its advocates to talk and sometimes act as if the moral obligations to which they subscribe were more important than the current employment in useful occupations of their fellow-countrymen.

The inclination to treat Lancashire as a declining sector, and thus not worth too much trouble, is a failure to recognise some of the factors mentioned in Chapter 2. The increasing use of man-made fibres, the use of Lancashire-type spinning to produce yarns for the growing knitting industry, and the interchangeability for many purposes of knitted and woven fabrics —these factors were making the traditional distinctions less relevant. For the reasons that Courtaulds had decided that they must regard their business as embracing all fibres and all fibre-using activities, so also was it necessary for government policy to treat the textile industry as one whole, though the industry itself did not make that easy in its continued pre-occupation with sectional interests. Alas, the necessary changes did not begin to come about until much later.

The 1959 Cotton Industry Act

The 1959 Act was intended to reduce the excess capacity resulting from the decline of exports and the growth of imports, and to provide finance for re-equipment. Under its powers some £11.3M was provided in compensation for scrapping and £13.4M in re-equipment grants to modernise in order to improve the competitiveness of the reduced industry. It was hoped that the import position would become more stable as a result of voluntary limitations on exports on the part of Hong Kong, India and Pakistan; and the ending of the spinners' price agreements as a result of a judgement of the Restrictive Practices Court had made it more urgent to deal with excess capacity. But the government had no power to impose changes on the industry and the Act did nothing about structure and organisation. A report from the Estimates Committee in the 1961–62 session concluded that 'failing a speedy and satisfactory solution to the related problems of imports, marketing and the fuller use of plant and machinery, much of the expenditure incurred will have been to no purpose.' This melancholy conclusion was all too amply confirmed in Caroline Miles' study.[1]

The failure of the 1959 Act to achieve any fundamental change in the industry strengthened those who considered that the Lancashire section should be allowed to decline, and perhaps even to disappear in the long run. By this time, however (see Chapter 3) Courtaulds was beginning to play a more active role in the industry. In January 1964 arrangements were made for a meeting at which Sir Richard Powell, then Permanent Secretary at the Board of Trade, urged Courtaulds to prepare a memorandum putting forward the case for a new approach.

The need for protection

The essential argument then put forward by Courtaulds to the government was that a modern textile industry is one of high

[1] Caroline Miles, *Lancashire Textiles—A case study of industrial change* (National Institute of Economic and Social Research, 1968).

capital intensity that produces a high value added per person. Economic policy, looking to the future, should therefore recognise that this industry can contribute as much to economic growth and to exports as any other. Yet the conditions which are under the influence of government were not as favourable as those in other Western markets or for other UK industries. Notably in cotton, these conditions were inhibiting development; and in other sections, such as wool fabrics and clothing, they created a potential threat inimical to confidence. Government policy should be to create the conditions which would justify the investment necessary to enable the industry's potential contributions to growth and exports to be realised. This required conditions for all branches of the industry similar to those of other UK industries and of the textile industries in other Western countries.

So ran the argument. It became the main theme of all subsequent representations with which Courtaulds was concerned. An important embellishment was the corollary that, because of the unsatisfactory position into which the industry had been brought by past policies, it would be necessary to accept that the well-established case for giving protection to 'infant industries' must be valid for the newly equipped, potentially viable plants, at least for a sufficient period to overcome teething troubles and initial losses. The low costs and potentially low selling prices which are possible with capital-intensive equipment depend for their achievement on operating at or near full capacity. This takes time to accomplish, and needs a period of special protection in some form.

The case was supported by reference to Barna's paper 'The replacement cost of fixed assets in British manufacturing industry in 1955'[2] in which it was estimated that the fixed assets per person employed in cotton and wool textiles was £2710 compared with £1830 for all manufacturing. Several industries with lower capital intensity were shown to have substantial levels of tariff protection.

[2] *Journal of the Royal Statistical Society* Series A (General), vol 120 part 1, 1957.

	Fixed assets per head £	Typical UK tariff %
Motor vehicles, aircraft	1830	25–33
Other vehicles	1000	20
Mechanical engineering	1500	12
Electrical engineering	1110	$17\frac{1}{2}$
Drugs, toilet preparations	1600	15–25
Paints, varnish	1470	$12\frac{1}{2}$
Rubber manufactures	1750	24
Cotton, wool (mainly cotton)	2710	$17\frac{1}{2}$ and nil

Senior civil servants needed convincing. Later, in January 1969 when the Textile Council's report was being discussed, a table was provided to show the increase in capital intensity in the industry expressed in terms of fixed capital per employee.

		Fixed capital employee £
a	In 1960 it was said that a modern textile mill involved: (source Hodara at the Textile Council Productivity Centre)	2 500
b	Ormerod, at the British Association in 1962, said that a new integrated spinning, weaving and finishing plant would require:	6 600
c	In 1966 a re-equipment scheme for spinning and weaving of sheetings would have required:	5 215
d	1968—new spinning mill in N. Ireland involved:	9 600
e	1968—new Carlisle and Skelmersdale weaving mills involved roughly:	10 000
f	1969–70—Break spinning—20's yarn:	18 000

Sir Richard Powell, having read the Courtaulds paper (completed in April 1964), said that it would be difficult to take any action which appeared to restrict the exports of the less developed countries since HMG were leading the campaign to get other industrialised countries to take more, but he accepted that this would not preclude a decision not to increase import quotas until other major Western countries had approached the UK level. His personal inclination was to abolish the voluntary quota system and impose on textiles from the Commonwealth the same tariff as applied to imports from other sources, with the aim of providing a more stable background for new initiatives towards regrouping. Some satisfaction was felt when the Director of the Economic Research Unit at the Board of Trade (Mr J B Heath) was reported as

satisfied that there was no case at all for the cotton textile industry having tariff protection less than that of typical manufacturing industry—and in view of the competitive nature of the cotton industry he thought there might be a case for it having more (as some protection against market disruption from new producers overseas).

The Board of Trade asked for further copies of the memorandum.

At the same time that the Courtaulds memorandum was presented in April 1964, it was learned that the Cotton Board were also preparing a paper. However, this was to be concerned with the imports quota position after December 1965, and its impact would depend on a recognition by the government of the long-term viability of the cotton industry. Others in the industry therefore welcomed the Courtaulds paper which sought to demonstrate this. The Cotton Board paper, when seen four weeks later, paralleled the one from Courtaulds, but went further in speaking of a gradual dismantling of quantitative limitations, assuming acceptance of its main recommendation that there should be counteracting duties on imports from low wage countries to bring their prices up to a fixed percentage of 'fair domestic price.' A strengthening of the then existing quantitative controls was put forward as an alternative. The Cotton Board were more explicit than Courtaulds about the need for quantitative restrictions on imports of garments.

The new government: Labour's administration
By November 1964 there was a new government. Courtaulds had made its important Lancashire acquisitions and so the

April memorandum was redrafted. Import saving seemed a politically appropriate theme to stress with the new adminis-tration. The aim was defined as 'to obtain conditions to allow the UK cotton industry to operate in an environment similar to that in which cotton industries in other western countries operated'—requiring primarily an end to price disruption caused by Commonwealth imports. Several means could be envisaged, but the most straightforward would be to impose an import duty of the order of 15 per cent; this was recognised to be a direct contravention of the Ottawa agreements. It was considered that quotas would be needed for an interim period of five years or more.

In February 1965 there was a further conversation with Sir Richard Powell, who now was concerned with the period up to 1970; he appeared to be weighing up the respective merits of continuing the quota system, or of imposing a tariff on Commonwealth imports. In April a factory visit by more junior civil servants provided an opportunity to stress that 'Courtaulds expected to hear further from the Permanent Secretary on the question of a tariff on Asiatic Common-wealth cottons.' The Courtaulds official reported, 'It became clear to me that this was most unlikely unless we took some steps to precipitate it and that a letter to the Permanent Secretary might be the proper tactics.' The difficulty it seemed lay not in the logic of the case but in the immensity of the negotiating difficulties for

> HMG are deeply committed to helping the lesser developed countries. On cotton textiles they really have entered into pretty irreconcilable commitments . . . [A tariff] is in due course inevitable but it is clearly going to take a major effort to get it.

A memorandum was sent to the Permanent Secretary and to the Prime Minister of which the essential was

> . . . it seems to us that a system might be designed which would involve a surcharge or levy on cotton textile imports into the UK from countries participating in the global quota which would otherwise enjoy duty-free access—such funds

being earmarked for refund by HMG in some manner acceptable to the lesser-developed countries concerned.

In April 1966 an attempt was made to revive the discussion with the Board of Trade and the official drew a distinction between those who 'might take the view that the sooner the UK gets out of the business of producing textiles and leaves it to developing nations the better for all concerned' and those who 'accept that it would be reasonable that the textile industries should have, in practice, the normal amount of protection which is provided to UK industries as a whole.'

The Cotton Board presented another paper in October 1966 —'The Future of the UK Cotton and Allied Textile Industry' —criticising government slowness in acting against imports. The paper was still protectionist in tone—too much so, Courtaulds felt—and not consistent with the vigorous attitude of confidence being expressed by Courtaulds, for example in the Chairman's speech at Harrogate in 1965, 'Management Organisation and Structure—The Next Five Years.' The debate in December 1966 bringing the Textile Council into being was used by Lancashire and Cheshire MPs to give vent to the full rein of protectionist sentiments.

By January 1967 senior government officials were seeking an off-the-record discussion about Lancashire, the President of the Board of Trade having been highly incensed at a deputation which led him to feel that 'despite all the talk, attitudes in Lancashire are quite unchanged.' The President (Douglas Jay) asked for a meeting. He was being harried by Labour MPs who in turn were being harried by trade unionists threatening to disaffiliate themselves from the Labour Party. The President was reported as feeling that he had reached the end of the road so far as anything he could do, and he appeared to be wanting reassurance that it would 'blow over' if he sat tight and was firm. A dramatic increase in imports from Portugal had been the trigger for these heated exchanges. Courtaulds' comments were on the lines already indicated, as they were some fifteen months later when Douglas Jay, no longer in office and by then a non-executive director of Courtaulds, arranged for some of his Courtaulds colleagues to meet a group of ten Labour MPs to try to convey a more constructive tone than prevailed in Lancashire.

A short account of the quota system may be useful at this stage.

Import quotas

The structure of quota control on textile imports had three strands: the arrangements on cotton textiles which developed and extended from the voluntary control arrangements negotiated with Hong Kong, India and Pakistan in 1959–60; the bilateral quota arrangements with Sino-Soviet countries within individual trade agreements and subject to annual review; and the arrangements under the Anglo-Japanese Commercial Treaty of 1962.

The conclusion of arrangements with Hong Kong for a three-year limitation on exports to this country was achieved in the same year as the Cotton Industry Act 1959, and was followed by similar arrangements with India and Pakistan. The annual total imports from these three countries were limited to some 420 million square yards (about 20 per cent of domestic consumption) with some categorisation by product. Europe and the USA at the turn of the 1950s were also facing a growing volume of imports of cotton textiles from the Far East, and on the initiative of the USA in 1961 the principal importing and exporting countries under GATT auspices worked out a scheme whose stated objective was to reconcile their interests in allowing orderly controlled expansion of international trade in cotton textiles. This 1961 Short Term Arrangement was converted into the 1962 Long Term Arrangement. It was renewed after the first five years in 1967 for subsequent three-year periods, and it was due for re-negotiation or renewal again in September 1973. The most extensive use of the LTA has been made by the USA, and this has to a large extent exposed its ambivalent purpose.

Because in the early 1960s imports into the UK under its own arrangements were so high, with a higher proportion of consumption than any other major importing country, the UK was absolved from operating the 5 per cent annual growths provisions of the LTA. The peak UK imports in 1964 showed up the weakness of the finger-in-the-dyke approach to quota controls renewed with the major suppliers and extended in a patchwork fashion to a few other countries in the interval. But it was not until January 1966 (on the basis of average 1962–64 imports) that the UK government introduced a system of 'global' quotas on imports of cotton yarn, fabric and made-up products from all sources except Europe, North America and generally the developed Commonwealth, continuing within the framework special quotas for Hong Kong and India.

The Textile Council's work
By early 1967 the study which had been initiated by Sir Richard Powell's letter of 6 June 1966 was under way. The key passages in that letter were:

We have now reached a position in which we can reasonably hope to hold imports from what can broadly be called low-price sources at a stable and predictable level for the next five years.

An assurance of a breathing space of this kind was regarded by the industry and accepted by the Government as necessary to enable progress towards the goal of a compact and viable industry to be continued and, indeed, accelerated. But it has not been easy to secure this breathing space and we have taken serious risks in achieving our objective.

It is therefore essential that the industry should make the best possible use of the time that has been bought; and I am writing to suggest to you that the Cotton Board should take the initiative in a major study of the ways in which the efficiency and productivity of the industry can most rapidly be increased. In doing so, the Board would be undertaking in many respects the functions of the Economic Development Committees which are engaged in similar studies for the industries for which they have been established. Since the Cotton Board possesses a unique background of knowledge and statistical information about its industry, it is in a specially favourable position to carry out this work.

I would hope that the Government would be associated

with the study, and the Board of Trade would be ready to work closely with the Cotton Board and to make available any information which it can properly provide.

The object of the exercise, as I see it at this stage, is to reconsider, in the light of all the information available, what are the obstacles to an increase of productivity in the industry and what measures can be taken, whether by the industry itself or by calling on available Government services, to reduce or eliminate them.

I use productivity here in a wide sense, to cover the use of well paid labour to operate advanced machinery, in such a way as to make the industry an effective part of the industrial base of a country that is short of manpower and must depend for its future on a massive increase in its rate of technological progress.

The Cotton Board, to which the letter was addressed, had been reconstituted as a development council under the 1947 Industrial Organisation and Development Act. It included representatives of both employers and unions, as well as independent members and an independent chairman, and it was financed by a statutory levy (extended in 1960–61 to cover man-made fibre-using activities). Partly because of its past history, the cotton industry was the first to be tackled under the 1947 Act, and by 1965 it was the last but one development council to survive. The Board had been empowered under the 1959 Act to prepare reorganisation schemes covering the elimination of excess capacity and the payment of re-equipment grants. In 1965 Courtaulds, ICI and Viyella were invited to send representatives to all policy-making meetings of the Board 'to bring into its counsels as far as possible the three organisations which have been responsible for substantial changes in the structure of the industry. . .'

In 1967 manmade fibre production and other activities were brought formally within the Board's ambit, and it was reconstituted as the Textile Council, though other sections (especially wool and hosiery) were still unwilling to participate. There was a substantial body of opinion in the industry which was in favour of extending the Council to cover all textiles, because of the increasing use of man-made fibres, the development of new processes, the increasing part played by firms with wide-ranging interests in textiles—but there was no unanimity. This was the Council responsible for the industry study.

Three project committees were set up, one with the title 'Economics & Statistics' with Mr W T Winterbottom as its chairman. He had been chairman of one of the Lancashire companies acquired by Courtaulds and was by this time an executive director of Courtaulds. Mr A M Alfred, Courtaulds' Chief Economist, was a member. Other members of this committee who played a major role were Mrs Caroline Miles, independent member of the Textile Council, and Mr S Stewart, one of the senior civil servants most closely concerned with the industry. All four were members of the editing committee which, in mid-1968, took over the results of the project committee's work. From the outset Courtaulds regarded this as the key committee. Final drafts of the full report were ready in January 1969 and it was published in March. The minister concerned stated in the House of Commons on 14 December 1971 that 'The comprehensive study leading to the tariff was one of the best studies of that sort into an industry.'

It was concluded that production costs in spinning and weaving were higher than those of competitors in both developed and developing countries because of high labour costs, despite low wages. There was a wide spread of efficiency within the industry. Since 1957 the number of production units had declined by a half, but high-cost firms had survived. There was surplus capacity and low-cost firms had been insufficiently aggressive in their price policies. The high level of imports had been partly responsible for hesitancy in re-equipping and restructuring, and in 1968 imports from developing countries were 40 per cent of consumption, compared with 10 per cent in EEC and USA where all imports were subject to duty.

The USA had made restrictive use of the GATT Long Term Arrangements of 1962 and 1967, and 'certain administrative arrangements' were believed to inhibit imports into some other countries. It was foreseen that there would be little change in the level of production, assuming that the foreign trade balance would improve by 200 million square yards between

1967 and 1975, taking account of devaluation, the announced plans of bigger companies and the comparative cost studies which had been made. As a result of productivity improvements, the number of spinning units would be halved by 1975, with an even greater reduction in the number of weaving units. As a result of modernisation, conversion costs in spinning and weaving ought to fall by 25 per cent, to make UK fully competitive with EEC, to improve its position slightly compared with USA and to narrow the cost gap compared with the Far East. The industry would be unlikely to get ahead with re-equipment and reorganisation unless there were a confident belief that it had a future, and this required changes in government policy, in particular a tariff on Commonwealth imports, with a transitional reliance on quotas as well. Given the right conditions it was foreseen that four or five firms would account for over half the output.

The Chairman of Courtaulds in an article in *The Times* on 1 April 1969 commented, 'my own firm, and other large groups in the industry, did not need two years of study and £100 000 of research to be in a position to recognise the validity of these conclusions,' but as an exercise in consensus politics a lot had been achieved.

On 22 July 1969 Mr Crosland, then President of the Board of Trade, announced the government's decision to introduce a tariff on Commonwealth imports from 1 January 1972. This was seen in both government and industry as a fundamental and far-reaching change of policy. It marked the culmination of a prolonged dialogue with the government, first alone and then with the industry.

Courtaulds' support for this move was influenced in part by the prospect of UK entry into EEC which would necessarily require alignment to the EEC tariff system. It was, of course, noted that this system itself was reinforced by other administrative measures which had the effect of restricting imports from low-cost countries to a much smaller proportion of the market than that reached in the UK; and it was a natural expectation that alignment to the EEC system would produce similar beneficial consequences for the UK industry.

The acceptance of a tariff on Commonwealth cotton

imports was coupled with a decision to let the quota arrangements expire at the end of 1971 without the transitional period
of simultaneous quota and tariff protection recommended by
the Textile Council. Following intensification of industrial
opposition to this policy, via established Trade Association
channels and a vigorous *démarche* by the Textile Industry
Support Campaign motivated from Lancashire in the autumn
of 1971, the government (now Conservative) suddenly
reversed the decision of the previous Labour administration
to end quotas in December.[3] Protectionist sentiment in the
USA and the prospect of eventual assimilation with EEC
arrangements were also material to the change of heart. These
quotas were, of course, limited to woven cotton goods (all
products of 50 per cent or more cotton) and new problems
arose with increasing imports of fabrics made from minority
cotton blends with man-made fibres.

But there has been a continuing inclination to deal with each
problem as it arose with no apparent recognition that the interrelationships between one textile product and another are so
close and substitutability so great that a more comprehensive
policy might be needed.

The continuing debate between industry and government in
this field has related—except for the 1959 Act—to ways of
dealing with imports, and not to direct financial support.
Under the 1959 Act a total of £24.7M was provided under the
scrapping and re-equipment programme, and if all other
direct financial aid is included, such as that through IRC, the
total does not come to much more than £30M. This for a sector
of the industry employing 100 000 is in stark contrast with the
help provided in other situations, such as sums in excess of
£35M in an effort to sustain about 5000 jobs at Upper Clyde
Shipbuilders.

It also contrasts with the direct financial aid offered to their
textile industries by the governments of other developee
countries. Thus the Japanese government is reported in *Th*d
Times of 8 May 1971 to have made £158M available for
restructuring assistance, of which 60 per cent was offered in

---

[3] For the change in policy, see Edmund Dell's interpretation, *Political Responsibility and Industry*, p. 154 ff. (Allen & Unwin, 1973).

loans on favourable terms. This was less than six months after a request from the Japanese industry for support measures as a palliative against the anticipated US restrictions on Japanese textile exports; and the offer was increased at the year end to total some £250M. The Italian government passed an Act in late 1971 to make available some £132M in concessional loans at 4 per cent to firms in regions with a concentration of textile production, again to aid restructuring and reorganisation.

The difference between such specially designated assistance programmes and other general measures is not readily appreciated in public circles. So it arises that *The Times* in a leader on 20 January 1972 can say, 'Courtaulds has played a part in rationalisation in Lancashire—encouraged by the various grants that Whitehall has made available'; but this can refer only to the investment incentives which have been available to all firms in all industries and thus fall to be considered in a later chapter.

THE DELL COMMITTEE

In January 1969 Courtaulds announced their intention to make an offer to acquire English Calico (see page 63). The Textile Council Productivity Report had not then been published, and there had been no official reaction to the Monopolies Commission recommendation (in their report published in March 1968 and discussed in Chapter 6) that Courtaulds' further acquisitions in the textile and clothing industries should be subject to certain restrictions to be laid down by the Board of Trade. The Press did not fail to note that the Chairman of Courtaulds had given up the chairmanship of IRC only two weeks previously. There was, of course, power under the 1965 Monopolies and Mergers Act to refer proposed acquisitions to the Monopolies Commission, but this would have been inappropriate in these conditions. Indeed Courtaulds took legal advice and it appeared that under the terms of the Act, and having regard to the terms of Inquiry for the Monopolies Commission's report, the Board of Trade were under no obligation to refer to the Commission before deciding whether or not to let Courtaulds go on.

English Calico had been formed as a result of the merger of English Sewing Cotton (one of the parties to the original 1962 Northern Plan described in Chapter 3) and Calico Printers, a merger which was regarded at the time as an attempt to forestall a bid made by Viyella for ESC early in 1968. Its 1968 sales of £80M compared with Courtaulds' textile sales in that year of £236M. Courtaulds regarded English Calico's activities as complementary to its own. They had finishing capacity, which Courtaulds' weaving and converting expansions did not provide for, a chain of retail shops, a profitable business in USA offering a useful basis for financing expansion, and a substantial usage of polyester/cotton spun fabrics, mainly imported, but a potential market for Courtaulds. Also because of their profitable thread business in UK and USA, they were an important factor in dealing with Coats Patons (before July 1967, J & P Coats, Patons & Baldwins) whose own profits came largely from thread; indeed the two companies together dominated the world thread business. Coats Patons as big users of acrylic fibre had been working closely with Du Pont, Courtaulds' competitors, and were building up their worsted yarn spinning business (see page 56). Coats Patons were thus strengthening their bargaining position with Courtaulds, and it was reckoned that English Calico would be a useful counterweight.

A statement was made in the House of Commons on 6 February 1969 that in the government's view the structure of the industry should not be determined solely by takeover bids and market forces. The Textile Council's report was expected, and the President (Mr Crosland) would review its findings. Courtaulds had at his request withdrawn their proposal about English Calico so that this review could be comprehensive. At this time the Monopolies Commission's report was of course still under consideration by the government.

The Chairman of Courtaulds wrote to the President of the Board of Trade on 10 February 1969 saying that their restraint in not commenting publicly on the Monopolies Commission's report had led to an interpretation in some quarters that Courtaulds had been acting in a manner prejudicial to the public interest, and suggesting that other monopoly situations in the textile field should first be examined by the Commission to remove the prejudiced impressions about Courtaulds so that there could be the 'objective discussion which you are seeking.' This did not happen.

The Minister of State, Mr Edmund Dell, was responsible for reviewing the English Calico situation, helped by a small group which included the Chairman of IRC (by then Sir Joseph Lockwood) and the Chairman of the Textile Council. But by mid-April the group had not met as such, and Mr Dell was said to have a highly personal approach to the subject.

However, two of the senior Board of Trade officials sought a meeting on 20 February at which Courtaulds gave their reasons for the English Calico bid, the background to their nylon project in 1964 independently of ICI, and the frustration of their efforts to embark also on the manufacture of poly-esters which ICI had said would be the 'challenge direct.'[4] Courtaulds also stated that the bid for English Calico would be abandoned if no other competitive group, in particular Coats Patons, were allowed to acquire it.

The first meeting with Edmund Dell took place on 23 April with no others present from the government or civil service. The conversation covered the same topics as those in which the civil servants had been interested, except that Mr Dell asked questions also about merging the Courtaulds and ICI fibre activities, leaving the textile activities to operate independ-ently. Courtaulds expressed their willingness to make such a plan, but said that ICI had hesitations about it.

A second meeting took place on 30 June at which the President was present. He had the draft of a statement to be made in the afternoon. It had been decided that the five main firms—Courtaulds, Coats Patons, Viyella, English Calico and Carrington and Dewhurst (C & D)—were not to be allowed to merge and that no foreign company would be allowed to acquire any of them. This standstill was seen as not for all time but for a matter of five years. Courtaulds agreed to accept this conclusion. The government also decided that they did not need to take a view on the linking of fibre manufacture with

---

[4] For the part played by ICI in the discussion, it is interesting to compare the account of Edmund Dell, op. cit. 89 ff.

textile production, and Courtaulds interpreted this as an encouragement to go ahead with their own polyester project, something which they had not been ready to cope with until then. The President indicated that he had 'taken into account' the Monopolies Commission report, and thus disposed of an awkward situation.

This conclusion to the Dell Committee deliberations was regarded in some quarters as a success for Courtaulds, who were abandoning an acquisition which did not matter all that much to them if their rivals were also prevented from it, and who were being encouraged to embark on a project which ICI had tried hard to discourage. The government did indeed appear to be following the line indicated by the President in a reply in the House on 12 February 1969:

> I certainly agree with my Hon Friend that further rationalisation is necessary. On the other hand, I do not agree with him that we need still one more outside independent study. The industry has been endlessly studied and endlessly reported on; and now that we know the facts it is a matter of making up our minds.

THE LEVER COMMITTEE

The next development towards the end of 1969 followed on reports that Viyella, one of the five companies covered by the standstill, was in difficulties. They had backed polyester/ cotton blend fabrics heavily and were said to have 'warehouses full of the stuff' with adverse effects on their liquidity. The Chairman was refusing to see anybody in Whitehall and was saying that the Dell report had stopped him from making an advantageous deal with one of the big American groups. There were rumours of dissension amongst the directors.

Viyella had received considerable financial support from ICI, though by this time there was no important financial relationship. However, Viyella was a major customer for ICI fibres and, with C & D, probably accounted for about 50 per cent of ICI's filament yarn sales in the UK. The rumours about Viyella received dramatic confirmation in the sudden announcement on 12 December 1969 that Mr J Hyman, who had built up the business, was no longer its Chairman.

On 23 December, ICI announced their intention to make an offer to acquire Viyella, and would then seek to merge that company with C & D. This appeared at first sight to represent an abrupt reversal of ICI's oft-repeated policy of avoiding a vertical structure and encouraging fibre-using firms through selective minority shareholdings. One textile industry executive unconnected with the companies directly involved considered that the main factors which had influenced ICI were the competitive encroachments in the UK polyester market, which had particularly disturbed licensees of the Crimplene trademark. Coats Patons as one of the licensees had recently acquired Heathcoats with a Hoechst licence which was worth more to the Coats Patons Group than their Crimplene licence; and similarly Qualitex had acquired Klinger who had a Hoechst licence; and Courtaulds had announced polyester plans.

The government announced on 13 January 1970 that a working group in the Ministry of Technology under the chairmanship of Mr Harold Lever, Paymaster General, would consider the structure of the textile industry in the light of the ICI initiative, assisted by (among others) Edmund Dell, now Minister of State at the Department of Employment and Productivity, the Chairman of the Textile Council and the Chairman of the IRC.

Courtaulds were told by ICI of their intentions, and representatives of the two companies later met on 2 January to consider their relationships. It was noted from the ICI side that Courtaulds was consistently one of ICI's three largest customers, and that their competence in textiles benefits an industry vital to ICI's fibre, dyes and chemicals; nevertheless the two companies live in a state of mutual suspicion and occasional open conflict. Various courses of action were put forward for consideration. From the Courtaulds side it was noted that in 1962, 1964 and 1966 ICI had refused to consider an all-fibre company, so Courtaulds had got on with building a vertical structure; that their profit record was better than that of ICI; that ICI's policy of acquiring minority holdings in textiles had failed; and that of the various possible courses a total merger was the most desirable, and the Lever Committee should be told so.

A version of this discussion was reported in the Press, and no further talks took place at this time. It then began to appear as if ICI would try to persuade the Lever Committee to seek ways of splitting Courtaulds' fibre from its textile activities. A senior director of ICI was reported as saying: 'In the US the Government makes it quite clear that vertical integration in the manner adopted by Courtaulds in this country is illegal. We only wish the Government would adopt the same policy here.' In fact the protected US domestic market had long provided the environment in which large, diversified and vertical fibre-using firms had been built up (Burlington, J P Stevens, UMM) many years before the explosive growth of the man-made fibres in the 1950s, so that US fibre producers had no further incentive to integrate forwards. Indeed, American Celanese, which had followed the same path as British Celanese, voluntarily divested itself of its fibre-using activities in the 1950s for good commercial reasons. A senior legal adviser was despatched to the USA to check the accuracy of Courtaulds' understanding.

Courtaulds met Harold Lever and others on 15 January. The company representatives said they would accept a continuation of the existing standstill on acquisitions, but that if ICI were to acquire C & D and Viyella it would be impracticable to remain quiescent; and something would have to be done to improve working relations between Courtaulds and ICI.

Others indicated privately what they proposed to say to the Lever Committee about the ICI proposal, which in general aroused little enthusiasm.

On 25 March the House were told that ICI's proposals would not be referred to the Monopolies Commission and would be allowed to proceed subject to certain undertakings. These included promises from ICI to reduce their shareholding in the combined company to not more than 35 per cent as soon as practicable, and if this had not been completed within twelve months, not to exercise more votes than if they had, and not to use their shareholding to influence the companies in their choice of fibres.

In his comments to the Press, Harold Lever stressed that with a 35 per cent holding ICI would not be able to influence fibre choice, and made a considerable feature of ICI's good faith.

It was also said that a code would be drawn up, in consultation with the fibre producers, designed to prevent unfair trading in fibres. The proposed code of practice was circulated for comment on 27 April 1970, but the industry considered it impracticable and based on a misconception of the market position. The House was told on 29 March 1971 (by the Minister—now Conservative) that 'since a code would be likely to limit the freedom of producers and users alike to respond to market forces, I have concluded that it would not be helpful.'

Later, in September 1971, ICI received permission also to acquire four of its major yarn customers—Qualitex and three Carrington Viyella subsidiaries, all licensees under the ICI-owned patents for the texturising of polyester yarn and thus members of the so-called 'Crimplene Club.'

HOW EFFECTIVE?

The Textile Council Report of 1969 is interesting as the most important example of government–industry relations considered in this study. The partial acceptance of its conclusions, though not creating an adequate basis for continuing viability of the Lancashire section of the industry, at least reflected a refusal to acquiesce in its decline and a willingness to aim at its viability.

From one point of view the episode can be looked at as a way of handling relationships. The Lancashire industry's methods of stating its case were failing and, as it appeared to Courtaulds, its eventual disappearance was inevitable. Large-scale acquisitions, a commitment to substantial new investment and an expression of confidence were needed to change government attitudes. The response to Courtaulds' actions appeared to confirm this analysis, as did the President's anxiety for reassurance on being newly faced with pleas for help along traditional lines which appeared to belie the Court-aulds' more positive stance. The senior civil servant saw what change in government policy would be needed, and that this would require convincing arguments and powerful backing. To abandon the Ottawa commitment of 1932 would not be an easy decision. The invitation to the Textile Council, with its employer and trade union membership, was a way of putting to the test what Courtaulds had been saying and of ensuring that the conclusions would carry weight; and to associate civil servants with the study gave some assurance that the case as presented would stand up to probing, and provided a continuing insight into its progress.

The episode can also be viewed more substantively. First, it failed to achieve the required degree of protection, partially recognised in the decision subsequently to extend the quotas. Secondly, it gave credence to views about the industry's structure which, combined with the effects of the Monopolies Commission report, influenced the work at least of the Dell and the Lever Committees.

An early move was to encourage the formation of groups of smaller firms in Lancashire to act as a counterweight to the influence which Courtaulds was thought to be achieving and to help prepare the industry for the post-1971 situation which would be quota-free. Consultants were employed by the Industrial Reorganisation Corporation to foster this process, which also offered financial support. In the event the results were negligible.

The reduction in the number of mills in the Lancashire section of the industry can be compared with the figures in the Council's report, recognising that these were simply 'statistical possibilities and must be regarded as illustrative rather than definite estimates.' The report's figures for 1975 implied reductions by 1971 which can be compared in the table over-leaf with those which took place.

The increased pace of change in 1971 is marked, though the reduction of units in weaving is well below the figure given in the report; and it is only in spinning and finishing that, as fore-seen in the report, three or four firms account for at least 50 per cent of the output—modest though that degree of concentration might now appear.

	Reductions implied by 1971	Reductions actual to 1971 (three years)	Reductions in 1971
Spinning	29	27	16
Weaving	110	96	37
Finishing	34	43	19

In practice the Lever Committee had no effect on what would have happened anyway, apart from the ICI undertakings which, given the facts of the power residing in ownership, might be of diminishing impact with the passage of time. The government's attempt to influence structure following the Textile Council report achieved nothing. So the Dell Committee was responsible for the only identifiable government influence on structure in dissuading Courtaulds from going ahead with the English Calico bid.

In improving protection against imports and so the conditions for viability, however, the activities described in this chapter had a positive—though limited—influence.

THE MANAGEMENT OF GOVERNMENT–INDUSTRY RELATIONS

In dealing with the matters discussed in this chapter, Courtaulds' relations with government were generally direct, although supplemented by selective participation in the work of the appropriate trade organisations. The arrangements for the Textile Council study itself have been described and appear to be a major exception to this general statement, but both in the preliminary policy discussions and in expressing views on the conclusions the senior management of Courtaulds were more conscious of their personal links with those who made policy, as is implied in the Chairman's unenthusiastic comment on the publication of the Textile Council's study.

Of these personal links it would be difficult to say whether those with ministers or those with senior civil servants at or near Permanent Secretary level were viewed as the most important. In dealing with the Textile Council study Sir Richard Powell's major role is apparent, though other senior civil servants were involved in discussion from time to time. In dealing with the Dell and Lever enquiries direct contacts with the ministers were more prominent, though senior civil servants were involved both in joint meetings at which ministers were present and alone.

From the Courtaulds side the Chairman was present at almost every senior level discussion which took place, and was often accompanied by one or more of his directorial colleagues.

The discussions were of many kinds—formal meetings in Whitehall offices and relatively informal meetings bringing together interested parties outside the normal working day. No one channel of communication predominated.

But parallel with these encounters were the day-to-day exchanges between the civil servants concerned with the textile industry, at Under Secretary level and lower, and the Courtaulds executives at the London head office who were concerned in every topic with which this volume deals. There was usually a dual process of communication, things which were said at the senior level meetings becoming the subject of confirmation, expansion and clarification in these other exchanges—often in the form of letters and memoranda.

The demands of the Textile Council study itself were such that those, including the civil servants, who were members of the key working party lived and worked closely together as colleagues for months.

It is difficult to generalise about the extent of the understanding displayed in these many contacts. Certainly in relation to any specific issue with which government had been directly concerned—tariff or quota arrangements, for example —those concerned on the government side were always well briefed. And when it appears that civil servants were failing to appreciate the importance of dealing with the whole rather than with part—as for example in the willingness to discuss quotas on polyester-cotton blend fabrics but not quotas on competitive viscose-cotton blend fabrics—intradepartmental problems might be more a factor than any failure of intellectual understanding of the point at issue.

But on more general issues relating to the conduct of a business enterprise there were occasionally some disconcerting responses, for example on the part of the senior civil servant who expressed great interest and surprise that the cash flow from fibres would go towards financing the Lancashire weaving project. And this lack of knowledge about the totality of a firm's strategic and financial behaviour may account for problems such as those arising from the limited nature of the Monopolies Commission reference to be discussed in the following chapter.

Chapter Six

GOVERNMENT AND COURTAULDS— SPECIFIC INTERVENTIONS

This chapter is concerned with government regulatory and control activities during the period 1960–70 in situations which were specific to Courtaulds.

As an appropriate introduction, the first to be mentioned is the ICI bid in 1961–62 which, although it did not provoke any intervention at the time, had important consequences in terms of government action; it influenced the drafting of the 1965 Monopolies and Mergers Act, which in turn influenced the handling of most of Courtaulds' subsequent acquisitions and in particular provided the legal basis for two major interventions (the Dell and the Lever Committees) discussed in the previous chapter.

Then came the reference in July 1965 of cellulosic fibres to the Monopolies Commission, and later references to the National Board for Prices and Incomes: each of these independent bodies established under legislation investigated situations according to given criteria, recommending to the government on specific lines of action, with the government then making its decision. They concentrated upon the structure, behaviour and performance of Courtaulds as an enterprise, and in effect—though not in the legal form of the inquiry—their centre of focus was the individual firm in its industry environment, and not the environment itself.

These 'enterprise specific' inquiries differed from the 'industry specific' Textile Council situation discussed in the previous chapter. In the latter the initiative lay as much with the industry as with the government, and the prolonged investigation and debate involved all interests—including government—with a stake in the Lancashire section of the industry. They differed also from the Dell and Lever inquiries which were set up *ad hoc* for narrow specific purposes, with no prescribed formal decision structure, yet again with the centre of focus in each case on the textile industry.

GOVERNMENT AND THE ICI BID

In December 1961 the House was told that the government had no powers to intervene in the attempted takeover of Courtaulds by ICI. However, the matter was raised again when Mr Erroll, then President of the Board of Trade, was asked (on 23 January 1962 by Douglas Jay) whether he would set up a public inquiry into the effects on the public interest of the proposed merger between ICI and Courtaulds. In a statement a week later the President pointed out that ICI and Courtaulds each had a sufficient share of the market for man-made fibres to bring it within the terms of the 1948 Monopolies and Restrictive Practices (Inquiry and Control) Act, that a merger would bring about a combination of exceptional size by UK standards, but that size alone could not be the criterion for reference. The 1948 Act was based on the policy that monopolies must be judged by their actual effects in practice, and that conclusions could not be reached until a monopoly had come into existence and there was experience of its working; and there was no reason to depart from this policy. The existence of competition from other countries, the presence in the UK of subsidiaries of large foreign companies, and the fact that users could apply for a tariff reduction were all cited as supporting considerations.

A House of Lords debate took place on 1 February 1962, as well as a debate initiated by Douglas Jay in the House of Commons on 14 February 1962 in which he advocated that there should be a regular system of investigation before mergers occur. The President indicated that a comprehensive review of policy concerning monopolies and restrictive practices was under way. This was not expected to be completed before the end of 1962, and the views of industry and other interests were to be sought. Although nothing was done at the time, the Courtaulds–ICI events of 1961–62 clearly influenced attitudes, and in the second reading debate on the 1965 Monopolies and Mergers Bill, both Douglas Jay and Edmund Dell made references to that situation.

THE MONOPOLIES COMMISSION

Background to the Courtaulds reference

Before 1948 no legislation existed in Britain for the regulation of monopolies and restrictive practices, although the existence of restrictive practices was noted in several official reports published in the inter-war period and in the mid-1940s. The 1944 White Paper on Employment Policy noted the growing tendency towards combines and agreements seeking 'to control prices and output, to divide markets and to fix conditions of sale.' The government's intention to seek powers in this regard led to The Monopolies and Restrictive Practices (Inquiry and Control) Act 1948.

Over the next few years the investigations conducted by the Commission made it clear that government concern was much more with restrictive agreements of one sort or another which might be endangering competition, than with dominant enterprises. In six of the ten cases found against the public interest (out of a total of thirteen investigations by 1956) the Commission criticised in detail such practices as the restriction of production by quotas, discriminatory pricing and the concerted fixing of prices. The Commission were therefore asked to undertake a general inquiry into several specific kinds of 'collective discrimination.' The Report (Cmnd 9504, 1955) identified six categories as most harmful to the public interest, broadly summarised as collective boycott, exclusive dealing and aggregated rebates; the Commission believed that there may be some situations where these practices may not be against the public interest, but during their inquiry they did not discover any instances in which they were clearly satisfied that such practices were beneficial. The government was greatly influenced by this Report, and the 1956 Restrictive Trade Practices Act was the direct result.

The Act introduced the presumption that certain restrictive

E

agreements were against the public interest, unless the parties could show that they were not. There were set out a number of beneficial effects one at least of which must be present before consideration could be given to the balance between any possible detriment to competition and the public advantage claimed.

The scope of action of the Monopolies Commission was thus much reduced by the Act, and was thereafter limited to investigation and report at the request of the Board of Trade on dominant enterprises and on restrictive agreements relating exclusively to the export trade, where the parties supplied at least one-third of the market, as defined in the Act, for the goods concerned. The Commission's membership was reduced to ten from twenty-five. By 1961 it was noted in the Press and elsewhere that the Monopolies Commission had become more or less moribund as a result.

In an opposition censure motion on economic policy (February 1961) Douglas Jay said:

> The irony of the situation is that the Restrictive Practices Act itself has actually in some degree incited the rush towards monopoly, because big firms now find that they cannot make a price agreement but they can amalgamate. I believe that in the case of Courtaulds and British Celanese—and it is natural from the firm's point of view—that was one of the decisive motives.

Argument was building up to the effect that the rush towards monopoly due to the increasing number of mergers should be stopped unless they had been judged by some public authority to be in the public interest. The review put in hand in 1961 was followed in March 1964 by a White Paper, 'Monopolies, Mergers and Restrictive Practices' (Cmnd 2299) in which it was stated that government thought it would be wrong to introduce into the law any presumption that 'monopoly is in itself undesirable without regard to the conditions under which it operates or to the manner with which it conducts its business.' The same sentiment was applied to size. It was considered, however, that the law should be stiffened in some respects and that the factual investigation should be separated from the assessment of consequences in relation to the public interest, as two distinct stages of an inquiry.

On mergers, the government thought it desirable to make it possible to have cases investigated where possibly harmful results might be suspected. They proposed therefore that the Monopolies Commission should have the power to inquire into any proposed or recently completed merger which would result in a monopoly or increase the power of an existing monopoly. It was not expected that such an inquiry would often be necessary, but in that event and if there was a finding against the public interest, the government would take powers to stop a proposed merger, or to dissolve one that had been completed.

Around this time the Conservative government were displaying no doubts about the benefit of Courtaulds' acquisitions. In reply to a Parliamentary question directed against the expanding control of Courtaulds and Viyella in the 'cotton' industry, Mr David Price, then Parliamentary Secretary at the Board of Trade, said:

The activities of the two companies concerned have so far done a great deal to modernise and thereby strengthen the structure of the industry. The latest bids by Courtaulds seem to me to be directed towards furthering and not impeding verticalisation.

During the Parliamentary debate on the White Paper, the Opposition argued that all mergers above a certain size should require Board of Trade approval. Furthermore, Douglas Jay, who had after the 1964 election become President of the Board of Trade, stated his belief (in a letter of 4 May 1965 to Sir Peter Runge, at that time President of the Federation of British Industry) that a shift in policy emphasis was necessary on monopolies and said that 'the mere absence of complaints does not necessarily demonstrate that all is well.' He denied, however, that references would be directed against 'size as such.' In the March debate on the Second Reading of the Monopolies and Mergers Bill[1] Mr Jay had said, 'Where a firm

[1] This Bill was based on the 1964 White Paper with modifications made by the new Labour Government after the General Election of October.

is really dominant in an important industry, controlling perhaps over half the market, I think that perhaps an investigation should usually be made whether or not there have been complaints of monopoly abuse.' Edmund Dell took an even stronger line, saying: 'We should start with the idea that private monopoly is bad, not only if its actions directly oppose public interest but if it fails to take full advantage of its size and efficiency to promote its own efficiency to its research and its exports. We should require from any monopoly the most rigorous and continuous justification for its existence.' He proposed regular accountability to the Board of Trade on indices of efficiency.

The list of suggestions received by the Board of Trade from individuals or bodies outside the government during 1961 for possible reference to the Monopolies Commission included for the first time 'rayon yarn' and 'cellulosic acetate tow' (as well as nylon yarn which had been suggested on an earlier occasion). The next year 'man-made fibres' was suggested under the heading 'Monopoly as Cause or Effect of Mergers' (Annual Report by the Board of Trade for the year ending 31 December 1962, Monopolies and Restrictive Trade Practices Acts 1948 and 1953).

The cellulosic fibre reference
On 2 July 1965 the Supply of Man-made Cellulosic Fibres was referred to the Monopolies Commission, under section 2 of the 1948 Monopolies and Restrictive Practices (Inquiry and Control) Act. The intention of the Board of Trade to make the reference was announced on 3 June, together with the intention to make three other references (flat glass, aluminium semi-manufacturers and electrical wiring harnesses for motor vehicles).

Courtaulds were warned at midday on 2 June 1965 of the intended reference, and an internal minute by Mr H R Mathys, the Deputy Chairman concerned, reads:

Subsequently I telephoned Sir Richard Powell and expressed our concern that this should be done at this particular time of increasing competition in the man-made fibre field and that one group of man-made fibres alone should be selected. Sir Richard emphasised that the proposed reference was in keeping with the statement of Mr Jay in the House during the Second Reading debate on the Monopolies and Mergers Bill when he said that companies which accounted for more than half the market in a particular product might be referred to the Commission without any complaint having been made against them; that it was in no circumstances an allegation of malpractice by Courtaulds Ltd and indeed no stigma should attach to Courtaulds; that he recognised it would involve a good deal of work on our part; but the Board of Trade was being pressed strongly to make more use of the Monopolies Commission. He said if I wished he would endeavour to fix a meeting with the President, and at my request he did so.

On Thursday 3 June I went to the President's Office at 12.30 p.m. as arranged. The President was still at the Cabinet meeting and I had about ten minutes' discussion with Mr C M P Brown and Miss M Dennehy, the two senior officials of the Board of Trade concerned with the man-made fibre industry and the Monopolies Commission respectively. As one was taking notes I repeated my general theme and received much the same reply as I had had from Sir Richard. During the discussion the President himself arrived and I repeated my points to him.

He listened most politely and in every way appeared to be sympathetic, even at one moment putting in a point on my behalf of how pleased the Board of Trade were to see the work we were doing in Lancashire. Nevertheless it was abundantly clear to me that the matter had been settled and nothing I could say would have any influence on the decision. I put this specifically to the President and he said he was, in fact, listening carefully and would consider what I had said and it was not impossible that there might be some change, but he finished off with a good political statement which in fact meant the decision had been taken before we were informed and it was not intended we should have any chance to modify it. In the course of the discussion with the President and the two officials the possibility of bringing in some reference to the other man-made fibres at the time of settling the Terms of Reference was raised, but when I pushed this point it was clear that it could not be, in their mind, an extension of the inquiry to cover all man-made fibres.

The main events

A Steering Committee of four was set up within Courtaulds with Mr Mathys as chairman and a panel of six officials, including the head of the Government Relations Department, a senior accountant and a senior member of the Legal Department. It was foreseen that some of these would spend most of their time on the inquiry. Experience of other firms had shown the importance of one or two key people examining in detail every paper submitted. It was necessary later to increase the number of full-time staff. Few formal meetings were foreseen. In the event the Steering Committee met on twelve occasions beginning on 24 June 1965 and ending on 27 September 1966. Junior Counsel attended for the first time on 21 December 1965 and Leading Counsel (D. A. Grant, QC) on two occasions (17 February and 1 March 1966)—though in the event D. A. Grant, QC did not handle the case and R. A. MacCrindle, QC took his place. The initiative of course lay with the Commission.

The normal procedure of the Monopolies Commission evidently falls into four main stages:

1   Informal stage—seeing representatives of the industry, explaining and discussing future procedure; discussing with the industry the best way to approach the collection of statistics—especially on costs; visiting factories to learn something of the processes.

2   Factual stage—collecting and cross-checking facts and figures by questionnaire, correspondence, interview and examination of records; written and oral evidence, closing with the Clarification Hearing solely on facts.

3   Public interest stage—beginning with notification of provisional finding that 'the (monopoly) conditions prevail,' together with perhaps some possible lines of criticism; written reply and hearing.

4   Report stage—examination of provisional findings, further information, and provision of an opportunity for the industry to comment on all relevant points.

In the cellulosic fibres reference, the history of events over more than a four-year period was as follows:

2 June 1965
Notice to Courtaulds of the intended Reference.
3 June 1965
Notice of Reference.
14 July 1965
Letter from the Commission with an invitation to a preliminary discussion of the Reference, and advising of an invitation to submit a memorandum describing and explaining (so far as relevant for the inquiry) the history, structure, organisation, production and distribution arrangements, relations with other companies and organisations in the industry, and any agreements or arrangements having a bearing.
30 July 1965
Meeting at the Commission.
August 1965
Monopolies and Mergers Act 1965 published.
December 1965
Sir Ashton Roskill took over from Mr Levy as Chairman of the Commission.
29 December 1965
Meeting with Commission's accountant.
March 1966
Memorandum submitted followed by answers to lists of supplementary questions.
28 September 1966
Letter from Mr Mathys to Sir Ashton Roskill on cost assessment.
3 October 1966
Letter from Sir Ashton Roskill noting that it is agreeable to Courtaulds for clarification hearing to be dispensed with—may be additional time for public interest hearing instead.
27 October 1966
Public Interest letter with three Annexes (factual, points for consideration and summary of customers' complaints)—

inviting written memorandum by 31 January 1967. Courtaulds said it would be impossible to submit the memorandum
—with the hearing at end-June—before March, and this was
eventually accepted by the Commission.

December 1966
At Courtaulds' request a list of favourable comments received
by the Commission was sent.

29/30 June and 6 July 1967
Public Interest Hearings.

13 December 1967
Informed that Inquiry completed and report sent to the
President.

5 March 1968
Report published.

22 July 1969
Announcement of government decision.

The evidence submitted in response to the Commission's
enquiries consisted of:

1   Replies to the Commission's questionnaire of 9 August
    1965, submitted in March 1966 and comprising 190
    printed pages.
2   A reply to the Commission's 'Public Interest' letter of
    27 October 1966, submitted in March 1967 and com-
    prising 212 printed pages.
3   Answers to supplementary questions between April and
    September 1966; a letter and a paper submitted by the
    company; accountancy information; and proofs of
    evidence on the particular developments chosen by the
    company for special attention.

After the Report had been published, in response to a Board
of Trade invitation, Courtaulds submitted a confidential
statement of seventy-eight pages, some extracts from which
are given later.

  The reader will appreciate that during the four years June
1965–July 1969, from the initiation of the inquiry until the
government announced its decision, the business of running
the company and implementing its policies (especially the

verticalisation moves described in Chapter 3) had to carry on regardless of the investigation. Indeed, the structure of Courtaulds was very different in July 1969 from what it had been in June 1965. On reading what follows, it is important to bear this in mind.

The main issues
The first organised course of action by Courtaulds was to engage on a programme of self-examination with a view to identifying areas of the company's business and history where it might be susceptible to criticism from the Commission. In particular it was felt that there were certain areas in which the Commission might draw conclusions which might—unjustifiably—be adverse to Courtaulds. No one person knew all the facts which had to be assembled before the Commission's questions could be answered authoritatively. Since the relevance of the earlier questions when they came was not always clear, there was an element of shadow-boxing. The areas identified for particular attention by the Commission were the acquisition of the small viscose producers, the Celanese merger, the technical exchange arrangements with EFTA producers, the verticalisation policy, and to a certain extent the relationship between ICI and Courtaulds and the ICI bid.

Throughout the presentation of evidence, discussion and a visit to factories arranged for the Commission members and staff, inter-fibre competition was given repeated emphasis by Courtaulds. In the memorandum submitted in reply to the Commission's questionnaire in March 1966 the theme was expanded into a few paragraphs illustrating the competitiveness between fibres. Courtaulds also expanded the theme of interdependence in the textile trade in reply to the Public Interest Letter in March 1967.

One motive in this was an attempt to have the Commission consider the Lancashire trading results as part of trade in viscose staple, necessary for a proper appraisal of profits on cellulosics. This was with the background to acquisition and investment in Lancashire, which had already been explained to the Commission as an act of faith not only in the Lancashire industry but in the future of cellulosics. Courtaulds had pointed out that it was virtually alone among world producers in believing in a future for the cellulosics: Du Pont, for example, had shut their staple capacity and were running down their viscose textile yarn capacity, and the European producers were concentrating investment in synthetics.

Inter-fibre competition was stressed throughout the evidence relating to pricing and production policies, particularly in the reply to the Commission's supplementary questions. The theme of inter-fibre competition and interdependence in the industry was later illustrated in an exhibition arranged for the Commission staff providing for two hours' viewing and making available specialist technical and commercial staff to explain the subject. It was the main theme which the company felt would not be self-evident to the Commission.

From about the middle of 1966 another issue was given prominence. This was the question of supply of acetate tow for the manufacture of cigarette filter tips. The subject was coloured by the situation which existed between Courtaulds and Eastman Kodak. Courtaulds had sought a compulsory licence to manufacture filter tips following earlier disputes with the Kodak subsidiary Cigarette Components Ltd as to the availability of acetate tow, during which Courtaulds successfully opposed two applications in 1964 and 1965 for duty remission on imported tow. It was apparent that the Commission had received a number of accusations from customers of supply shortage. Courtaulds knew that Cigarette Components Ltd, as the largest customer for cigarette tow and in view of the current relationship, would have presented the most bitter case. The general situation was aggravated by the fact that 1964–65 represented a time of peak demand for cellulosic fibres (except possibly for viscose textile yarn).

The Commission's questionnaire to Courtaulds' customers coincided with this. The Commission drew conclusions, therefore, that Courtaulds had undersupplied the market. There is little doubt that the snapshot view of shortage in 1965, created by the greatest textile boom since 1945, influenced their main conclusion that Courtaulds' production policy was contrary to the national interest. They described this as 'the limitation of supply to the level most advantageous to the producer which is below the level that would be met in a competitive situation' (para. 175).

The second list of supplementary questions from the Commission had shown them obsessed with the idea of perfect balance between supply and demand, and likely to be unappreciative of the cyclical variations peculiar to the textile industry. Because of the high degree of fragmentation in the industry, fluctuations in final demand become greatly amplified as stock changes take place in intermediaries; the supplies of the basic materials then become subject to situations of demand which are unrealistic in relation to the pattern of final consumption.

In an annex to the Public Interest Letter the Commission had set out a list of points arising for consideration, the chief of which were:

1 The reason for Courtaulds' dominant position.
2 Whether Courtaulds planned its production with regard to the interests of its customers and the textile industry.
3 Whether Courtaulds could determine its price policy to suit its own immediate interests.
4 Whether it had deterred others from competing.
5 The effect of the arrangements which had been made with producers in the EFTA countries.
6 Whether the intention in vertical integration had been primarily to secure tied outlets, and whether direct competition with customers and preferential treatment to subsidiaries was expected to be against the public interest.

These points drew together the strands in the Commission's thinking that had emerged in the earlier requests for evidence, particularly in the four lists of supplementary questions received between April and September 1966 to which replies were submitted in July and October. Courtaulds' replies to these public interest questions sought to demonstrate the competitive position of cellulosic fibres and of Courtaulds, in stressing again the positive steps taken to develop new fibres and to strengthen the industry. Courtaulds stressed that they were still in a highly vulnerable position and that absolute monopoly conditions could never obtain in a situation where competition from imported fibres, from synthetic fibres and from imported fabrics provided strong and continuing pressures. The pipeline problems created by fragmentation in the industry were again referred to with particular reference also to the increased purchasing power of large retail groups. The 'shadow boxing' at this point stopped, as the issues on which the Commission were concentrating became clearer.

Another way in which Courtaulds might be said to have tried to direct the Commission's thinking was in the offer to make available for cross-examination five key persons in the company from whom proofs of evidence were presented to the Commission before the Public Interest Hearing. Three statements (on carpet fibre, industrial yarn development and Tricel marketing) were positive efforts to persuade the Commission to recognise the company's achievements. The two others, on pipeline stocks and the smaller viscose producers, were evidence to refute allegations of action against the public interest.

A certain amount of information was contained in the initial evidence about research achievements especially in the development of new and improved cellulosic fibres for different end-uses. A detailed summary of Courtaulds' contribution to the technology in fibre to yarn and fabric conversion and in dyeing and finishing was appended. Although not much should be read into this, the Commission's summary of Board Minutes and Papers condensed references to research to one page, which included one paragraph of seven lines on the new cellulosic fibre types and end-uses. In the supplementary questions those relating to research were minimal. One of these related to Courtaulds' research policy in recent years. The company, in its reply, asserted that its role was in applied research, the more fundamental kind being the job of the universities. Detailed accounting information to illustrate productivity achievements was also submitted during the course of the inquiry at the Commission's suggestion.

Much of the evidence was necessarily defensive, but every

opportunity was taken from beginning to end to stress the company's achievements and to develop in every conceivable way the overriding theme of inter-fibre competition, and competition from other large international companies.

At the outset Courtaulds were advised by a former member of the Commission—by this time an employee of the company —that it was valuable if friendly relationships were built up between members of the Commission's staff and the people handling the case for the company. It was also urged that Counsel was essential at the Public Interest Hearing, though some cases had been damaged by a Leading Counsel who had not had sufficient time to brief himself.

The Commission's methods of working did not encourage any effort to achieve any such *rapport*. Indeed the flow of written questions in formal style, some with little apparent relevance to the issue, the polite but reserved reaction to any special submission which the company felt it necessary to make as the failure of understanding became apparent, the lack of any contact with members of the Commission except at formal meetings—all combined before the Public Interest Hearing to produce a sense of bafflement and frustration. The formality of that hearing, accentuated perhaps by the presence of Counsel, and the hostile tone of the questioning, increased the feeling of being completely misunderstood by those who were unable or unwilling to try to understand, long before the actual report appeared. Members of the Commission had too little time—one even said that he tried to allocate two hours every Sunday for his Commission work—and were thus slaves to the staff or their own preconceptions.

The recommendations and Courtaulds' response
The report was published on 5 March 1968.

The Commission found that the following were things done by Courtaulds as a result of or for the purpose of preserving the monopoly conditions:

1   The practice of supplying cellulosic fibres to certain customers on terms or under conditions which were not obtainable by those customers' competitors.

2   The regulation of imports of cellulosic fibres into the United Kingdom through arrangements with EFTA producers.
3   The policy of extensive participation in the textile industry.

The Commission concluded that the monopoly conditions might be expected to operate against the public interest, as did the practice of offering preferential terms and conditions to certain customers, the regulation of imports through arrangements with EFTA producers, and the policy of extensive participation in the textile industry.

The Commission recommended remedies which included that: import duties on cellulosic fibres should be reduced to 10 per cent for staple fibre and tow and 15 per cent for continuous filament yarn; Courtaulds should sell cellulosic fibres, whether to its subsidiaries or to other customers, only at its published list prices and terms and should give no preference to any customer either in price or otherwise in the supply of such fibres; Courtaulds should bring to an end those aspects of its arrangements with EFTA producers which allegedly restricted competition in the supply of cellulosic fibres in the United Kingdom; and that Courtaulds should not be allowed, without the permission of the Board of Trade, to make further acquisitions in any sector of the textile and clothing industries (including wholesale and retail distribution as well as manufacture) if its share of capacity (or of sales, as appropriate) in that sector exceeds a figure laid down by the Board of Trade or would do so following those acquisitions. The figure suggested as appropriate for manufacturing sectors was 25 per cent. In this latter recommendation the Commission went well beyond its terms of reference.

On at least one previous occasion the President of the Board of Trade had announced forthwith his acceptance of the Commission's recommendations, which in the event had proved inconvenient for all concerned. On this occasion, as a result of prior consultation, the President, after summarising the conclusions, confined himself to saying that he would institute a review of the tariff and would have discussions with the company.

Courtaulds decided to make no public comment and to concentrate energies on persuading the Board of Trade that the Commission had completely misread the position. It was apparent that the misunderstandings were so profound that this objective would take time to achieve. There would be advantage in taking as much time as the Department would accept in order to have the fullest opportunity for the arguments to be reinforced by external evidence about the real situation, which it was thought must become obvious to officials once their attention had been focused on the issues. The Textile Council's productivity study was well under way and it was thought also that its findings would materially influence attitudes towards the company. In the Board of Trade's letter of 19 March 1968, Courtaulds was invited 'to make any comments they wish on those sections of the report relevant to the proposal for the reduction of import duties.' Accordingly, a confidential statement was submitted, from which it is relevant to give some extracts.

The Commission's recommendation that import duties should be reduced was put forward by the Commission as a remedy for its central conclusion that the 'monopoly conditions' in cellulosic fibres 'operate and may be expected to operate against the public interest.' Hence whether the remedy was correct depends upon whether the central conclusion of the report was correct. Courtaulds disagreed with that conclusion (and so the remedy proposed) partly because it was based on assumptions which did not bear any relation to the facts before the Commission and partly because it ignored the wider factors which determine Courtaulds' business strategy as a fibres and textile company.

The main attack in the statement consisted in contrasting the favourable comments in the body of the report with the adverse conclusions and recommendations. Thus in para 217 the Commission states: 'We recognise that [Courtaulds' size as a producer] bring[s] significant benefits to the public interest, especially in the present state of international competition in fibres and textiles' (para 215). Later in the same paragraph, the Commission states 'in many respects we are impressed by Courtaulds' efficiency and success, and many of its customers are well satisfied with the service which it gives them.' This favourable view of Courtaulds was reflected in an earlier passage in the report in which the Commission stated:

We have already shown in reviewing the history of the industry in this country how a large producer is at an advantage over smaller competitors. Courtaulds' size as a fibre producer has brought substantial benefits to users and so to the public. Getting almost all the production of cellulosic fibres into its own hands gave it scope for cost reduction by eliminating surplus capacity and by planning production economically. The result of this, and of the improved production methods and plant which Courtaulds has introduced, has been an impressive record of rising productivity, and prices have been kept stable over long periods despite rising wages and raw material costs. Courtaulds' record in the development and marketing of new products such as tri-acetate and the improved carpet fibres and tyre yarns, has also been creditable, and an important factor in this has been the scale of the resources Courtaulds could put into development. In part, of course, these benefits could be regarded as a response to competition from other fibres, which has acted as a safeguard against the stagnation which could result from monopoly, but they would not have been practicable for a small company (para 199).

In its historical account of Courtaulds, the Commission states:

Having been far-sighted enough to see the possibilities of man-made fibres and to buy production rights under the master patents, Courtaulds made full use of the opportunity provided by this initial period of protection and proceeded to exploit the new fibres energetically. We think that it deserved much credit for this. Courtaulds' long experience in the textile industry assisted it materially, but in deciding to try to develop man-made fibres it was taking a step into a new and unknown field which must have required considerable courage and faith. Others in Britain entered the field only after Courtaulds had created the opening and shown that it could be profitable; by the time that they did so Courtaulds had a lead in technical know-how, in scale of manufacture and in marketing (para 150).

With regard to the pricing policy of Courtaulds, the Commission states: 'Its [i.e. Courtaulds'] price policy had the effect of passing on to the consumer the benefit of reduced costs and of widening the market for cellulosic fibres even while it discouraged others from entering it' (para 152).

With regard to the significance of inter-fibre competition, the Commission states: 'The history of cellulosic fibres tends to support Courtaulds' contention that the power derived from a monopoly in cellulosic fibres is limited by the competition of other fibres.' (Para 164.) Later, in para 165, the Commission states: 'Although therefore the competition [from other cellulosics] is small in extent, Courtaulds can reasonably claim that it is nevertheless selling in competitive markets.'

With regard to Courtaulds' profits, the Commission states: 'On this basis Courtaulds' profit rate [replacement basis] remained below the rate for manufacturing industry throughout the period 1960–67' (para 182).

With regard to Courtaulds' policy of vertical integration, the Commission states: 'We do not consider that on balance Courtaulds' vertical integration has so far acted against the public interest' (para 237).

Having drawn attention to these favourable comments, the Courtaulds' memorandum then dealt one by one with those paragraphs which were adverse. The detailed criticism of individual paragraphs is too lengthy for inclusion here, and not amenable to summarising. An example will indicate the general approach:

In the light of all the evidence we consider that the production policy pursued by Courtaulds exemplifies one of classic disadvantages of monopoly, the limitation of supply to the level most advantageous for the producer, which is below the level which would be met in a competitive situation. This has led to shortages from time to time and it is likely to result in a lower level of exports (or a higher level of imports) both of fibres and of products made from them than might otherwise be achieved (para 175).

On which the comment is made:

This paragraph is probably the most crucial to the Commission's conclusion. According to the latest publication of the FAO (United Nations) the per capita consumption of cellulosic fibres in the UK, USA and EEC has been:

	1963	1964
	(lb per capita)	
UK	6.8	7.9
USA	6.8	7.5
EEC	6.1	6.1

On that basis consumption in the UK is as high or higher than in other countries.

Similarly, as the following table shows, consumption of cellulosic fibres as a percentage of total consumption of all fibres, natural and man-made, is higher than elsewhere in the world. Cellulosics have also made more rapid progress in the UK since 1955 than in other countries.

Cellulosics as % of consumption of cotton, wool and man-made fibres

	UK	USA	EEC	World
1955	21%	21%	24%	17%
1967	27%	18%	22%[a]	19%[b]
Change	+6	−3	−2	+2

[a] Percentage based on 1966 data
[b] Percentage based on 1965 data

In the light of the above figures, it cannot reasonably be said that in the UK there has been a 'limitation of supply . . . below the level which would be met in a competitive situation'.

So far as exports are concerned, the record of Courtaulds in cellulosics is good by any standards, as the following table shows:

Courtaulds' export sales as a proportion of total sales (%)

	1966	1967
Viscose yarn	19	23
Acetate yarn	24	31
Viscose and acetate staple	24	35
Total all cellulosics	23	31

There were more than twenty such detailed criticisms of statements by the Commission, equally cogent and supported by appropriate statistical evidence. Then followed a criticism of the way in which the Commission had dealt with customers' complaints:

> In the UK the company has 487 customers for viscose staple, 850 for viscose textile yarn, 215 for viscose industrial yarn, 400 for acetate yarn, 30 for acetate staple and 3 for cigarette tow. Of those, it appears that 23 made criticisms of Courtaulds and a further 20 some criticisms combined with favourable comments. It would have been surprising if from that number of customers representing a large number of different industries and different end-uses no complaints had been made to the Commission.
>
> A list of vague, generalised criticisms appears in Appendix 14 of the Report and resembles that put to the company in Annex III of the Commission's Public Interest Letter. Neither the name, nor in most cases, the full text of the complaint was disclosed to Courtaulds. In one particular case (that of a Trade Association), the Association heard from the Commission that it was intending to extract and summarise certain criticisms which had been made of Courtaulds. It was so concerned that Courtaulds would thereby get a wholly distorted impression of the Association's evidence that it sent Courtaulds a copy. The impression given by the full evidence was quite different from the Commission's summaries.
>
> Nevertheless, despite the difficulty of dealing with complaints submitted in such a way, the company provided answers to each of them. It seems to the company to be most objectionable therefore that the Commission should reproduce in Appendix 14 a list of complaints without the company's answers to them. Some of these answers are dealt with generally in the text of the Report but many are not.

The second part of the critique on Courtaulds' business strategy suggested that the report was dominated by the concepts of atomistic competition which inspired the original legislation and continued with a quotation from Schumpeter:

> ... we are dealing with an organic process ... Every piece of business strategy acquires its true significance only against the background of that process and within the situation created by it. It must be seen in its role in the perennial gale of creative destruction; it cannot be understood irrespective of it or, in fact, on the hypothesis that there is a perennial lull. But economists who, ex visu of a point of time, look for example at the behaviour of an oligopolist industry—an industry which consists of a few big firms—and observe the well-known moves and countermoves within it that seem to aim at nothing but high prices and restrictions of output are making precisely that hypothesis. They accept the data of the momentary situation as if there were no past or future to it and think that they have understood what there is to understand if they interpret the behaviour of those firms by means of the principle of maximising profits with reference to those data. The usual theorist's paper and the usual government commission's report practically never try to see that behaviour, on the one hand, as a result of a piece of past history, and, on the other hand, as an attempt to deal with a situation that is sure to change presently—as an attempt by those firms to keep on their feet, on ground that is slipping away from under them.

It then continued with an account of the factors which had influenced the company's strategy from 1957 onwards. This has been described in Chapter 3. The final parts of the statement dealt with the more technical tariff matters, arguing generally that reduced tariffs should be part of negotiated arrangements giving compensating advantages in other markets, and not unilaterally reduced in isolation.

The civil servant concerned commented that the statement was 'a powerful piece.' It was followed by three formal meetings at the Board of Trade in March, May and December, and a separate series of meetings with the Tariff Division. The tariff discussions assumed quite a different tone from that of the meetings on the more general issues. The civil servants concerned with tariffs were conducting the kind of probing exercise with which they—and their Courtaulds counterparts —had been long familiar. The inevitable conflict situations between the public and the private interest need not lead to crises if there are known rules of the game and experienced players. The key point in these discussions was reached when the Courtaulds representatives were asked for a hypothetical assessment of the company's likely response to a tariff cut, particularly as to selling prices and the expected consequences for volume and profitability; and their refusal to be drawn was accepted as a legitimate response.

The Board of Trade suggested that Courtaulds should give an undertaking about the prices at which fibres would be sold or transferred. Courtaulds said this would be acceptable if other producers gave similar undertakings and if the Board of Trade were to police their carrying out; but it appeared there was no statutory basis for that. Eventually Courtaulds gave an assurance that it would not discriminate between its own subsidiaries and other customers in the supply of cellulosic fibres except on purely commercial grounds. The proviso seemed adequate to cover all situations likely to occur in practice. Courtaulds also agreed to terminate its arrangements with EFTA producers. On tariffs it was decided to make no major unilateral changes.

These conclusions were announced in the House on 22 July 1969, fifteen months after the Commission's report.

Although there were no major changes it was decided to reduce the tariff on cellulosic tow, the volume of which was quite small compared with that of staple. This decision was in part related to the acetate cigarette tow situation already mentioned. This had been further examined in a Monopoly Commission report on Cigarette Filter Rods, resulting from a reference in May 1967, with a report published on 23 July 1969 (the day after the Minister's announcement on the cellulosic fibre report). Courtaulds was the principal complainant but the Commission decided that there was nothing against the public interest. Profits on capital employed (historic basis) had been 40 to 50 per cent for some years, which was considered high but justified by the firm's skill in exploiting its opportunities in a high risk trade.

The duty on synthetic tows had also been under attack fairly regularly from the mid-1950s. Acrylic tow gave rise to particular problems. Courtaulds were receiving complaints about the quality of tops produced by independent top-makers using Courtaulds' acrylic fibre tow. Insufficient control during processing seemed to be the problem. It was decided to stop supplying the independent top-makers and they were informed individually in June 1967 after the Board of Trade official had been told informally. There were vigorous Press reactions and a question in the House of Lords asking the government to 'review anomalies' in import duties on synthetic fibres, whilst in the House of Commons the Minister in reply to a similar question hinted at a possible reference to the Monopolies Commission.

This was followed in March 1968 by an application for reduction of the import duty, formally on all man-made fibre tows (advertised at the same time as the Tariff Review into cellulosic fibre duties). After a meeting in November at the Board of Trade, and a five-month suspension of action on the matter at the applicant's request, it was resuscitated in May 1969. Eventually a letter from the Board of Trade in November announced that no further action would be taken.

The reduction in the cellulosic tow duty, announced in July as part of the decision taken by the government on the Monopolies Commission Report, operated from September. It was, therefore, the only duty reduction applied to man-made fibres outside the scheduled 'Kennedy Round' cuts.

Acquisitions

Discussion of the Commission's fourth major recommendation about acquisitions was overtaken by events, in particular Courtaulds' announcement of their intention to make a bid for English Calico. This was followed by the setting up of the Dell Committee, discussed in the previous chapter.

The administration of mergers policy, following the Commission's report

The setting up of the Dell Committee had important consequences for subsequent developments in the relationships between government, Courtaulds and ICI. Other acquisitions did not provoke such immediately far-reaching consequences. Nevertheless under the terms of the 1965 Monopolies and Mergers Act they called for consultations between Courtaulds and the Board of Trade and decisions by the latter whether to refer to the Monopolies Commission. Under the Act the Board of Trade needed to consider whether to refer if the assets taken over exceeded £5M or if the market share as a result of the acquisition were to exceed 33⅓ per cent. It soon became apparent that as a result of the Monopolies Commission report with its reference to 25 per cent as the sensitive point for market share purposes, Courtaulds were going to be subject to an additional test, at least so long as that report was under consideration.

There were, of course, the familiar arguments about which market was relevant, and at the time of the proposed acquisition of Derby & Midland Mills before the Commission had reported there is a letter (dated 28 September 1965) from the Courtaulds Commercial Director to the Commission's Secretary drawing attention to the interchangeability between warp knit and woven fabrics in a number of uses, and asking for a less obsessive preoccupation with Courtaulds' share of the warp knit fabric market.

The Courtaulds' staff at head office established an easy working relationship with the Board of Trade officials concerned with mergers, and made a practice of advising them informally of all likely acquisitions as soon as possible, even if they fell obviously outside the Board of Trade guidelines.

In 1966 a number of primarily hosiery and lingerie companies were acquired, of which only Kayser Bondor was above the £5M asset reference figure of the Act and therefore subject to possible reference to the Monopolies Commission. The decision not to refer the bid was given within ten days. For the rest the 'courtesy' notifications were confirmed within a few days in each case as being not within the terms of reference of the Act.

In 1967 a number of textile wholesalers were acquired, of which two (Bell Nicholson and Wilkinson Riddell) were within the terms of reference of the Act. In this period (May) Wolsey also were acquired, and Prew Smith early in 1968. The Wolsey bid and those for Macanie, Bradbury Greatorex and Larkins for the first time gave rise separately to detailed requests by the Board of Trade for information as to plans for integration (in the case of Wolsey) and of continued freedom of choice of suppliers (in the case of the wholesalers). In the case of Wolsey, confirmation that there would in fact be no reference was delayed for over three weeks by the Board of Trade, in spite of the President's encouraging attitude to rationalisation in the textile industry.

The bids for Clutsom and Kemp and for Northgate in January/February 1968 (both notifiable) were together confirmed as not to be referred to the Commission. Here again the detailed analyses of market shares and supply relationships caused three to four weeks to elapse from notification to clearance.

Then followed a number of acquisitions on which there was no formal obligation, either on market share or asset criteria, to notify the Board of Trade, but Courtaulds did so and on each occasion obtained confirmation within a week or so of non-referability under the Act.

The first notification of importance after publication of the Monopolies Commission Report, with the 25 per cent market share which the Commission had identified as 'dangerous,' related to the abortive discussions over Bear Brand, a stocking company. It was clear that the 25 per cent test would weigh additionally in the future, even though as a figure it was not part of the Monopolies Commission final recommendations and the Report had not yet been accepted by the Board of Trade.

When Courtaulds announced their intention to bid for Ashton Bros, the Board for the first time made public their decision not to refer to the Monopolies Commission by issuing a Press Notice. This referred to their responsibilities under the Monopolies and Mergers Act 1965 and to the implementation of the recommendations of the Monopolies Commission Report 'without prejudice to the ultimate decision to be taken on implementation.' Clearance took five weeks from notification. Board of Trade Press Notices were also issued relating to the acquisition of International Paints and of Moygashel in the same year (1968). The 'without prejudice' proviso was now a feature of the Board of Trade's confirmation not to refer bids to the Commission notably in the case of Rowley (July 1968) and of Moygashel (October 1968). Moygashel, being referable under the 1965 Act, again took three weeks for clearance.

This led to some irritation because Courtaulds were being encouraged to get on with integration, by both the Prime Minister in private conversation and the President of the Board of Trade (Douglas Jay), and the punctiliousness of the Board's officials contrasted oddly with this pressure.[2] The civil servant concerned with the textile industry reassuringly pointed out that it was necessary to obtain the requested information and this did not cut across the top-level policy of encouraging Courtaulds to get on with integration.

THE PIB REFERENCES

Outline of history
In December 1964, encouraged by the Rt Hon (now Lord) George Brown, then Minister in charge of the Department of Economic Affairs, employers' organisations and unions signed a 'Statement of Intent' undertaking to co-operate in keeping under review the general movement of prices and incomes and to examine particular cases to see whether they were in the national interest. In February 1965, the government published (Cmnd 2577) its proposal to set up a National Board for Prices and Incomes, better known as the PIB.

There had been a prolonged public debate during the preceding two years, beginning whilst a Conservative government was still in office.

The February White Paper was followed by another (Cmnd 2639) in March setting out the criteria for price changes.

---

[2] Edmund Dell confirms government approval of Courtaulds' policy of restructuring the industry. Op. cit. 90, 99.

Enterprises, it said, would not be expected to raise prices except:

1 If output per employee cannot be increased sufficiently to allow wages and salaries to increase at a rate consistent with the criteria for incomes stated in paragraph 15 below without some increase in prices, and no offsetting reductions can be made in non-labour costs per unit of output or in the return sought on investment.
2 If there are unavoidable increases in non-labour costs such as materials, fuel, services or marketing costs per unit of output which cannot be offset by reductions in labour or capital costs per unit of output or in the return sought on investment.
3 If there are unavoidable increases in capital costs per unit of output which cannot be offset by reductions in non-capital costs per unit of output or in the return sought on investment.
4 If, after every effort has been made to reduce costs, the enterprise is unable to secure the capital required to meet home and overseas demand.

The PIB's terms of reference and methods of working were also set out.

In September the government announced its intention to seek statutory powers to introduce compulsory notification of proposed changes affecting goods and services of particular economic significance, and in November were published (Cmnd 2808) the arrangements for an 'Early Warning System' listing goods for which there was to be a four weeks' advance notice of proposed changes and a further three-month period for inquiry if the government so decided. Textile yarn, thread and man-made staple fibre were included in the list. Then in July came a further White Paper (Cmnd 3073) laying down criteria more stringent than those of April 1965 with a standstill for the period to December 1966 and a period of severe restraint for the next six months to June 1967. The Act received the Royal Assent in August 1966 and Aubrey Jones, a former non-executive director of Courtaulds, became the first PIB chairman. (The writer was, for a while, a CBI nominee as a Special Member.)

The arrangements following January 1967 were set out in a

White Paper (Cmnd 3235) in March; generally the broader criteria of the April 1965 document were to operate. The 1967 Act (in July) supplemented the 1966 Act and gave powers to extend a standstill for six months from the date of a reference, but this was to expire in August 1968. A White Paper (Cmnd 3590) envisaged a standstill of up to twelve months after a reference, the criteria were to be those of the March 1967 document, and the early warning arrangements were to continue. The Act incorporating these arrangements was passed in July 1968, but the delaying powers were to expire at the end of 1969.

The man-made fibre and cotton yarn references

In February 1969 the PIB were asked to investigate viscose yarns, acetate yarns and cotton and man-made fibre yarns. The latter was handled with the PIB by the appropriate Lancashire trade association of which Courtaulds were naturally members, but Courtaulds decided to play no active part. The PIB report published on 17 October 1969 recommended that 'the Government should not attempt intervention to enforce price reductions.'

The viscose and acetate yarn references came at a time when Courtaulds were still involved in discussions with the Board of Trade about the Monopolies Commission report, when the Dell Committee had just been set up and the Textile Council Productivity Study was still under way. There was some natural feeling that Courtaulds were receiving more than their due share of attention and a tone of asperity appears in some of the exchanges which took place.

Viscose prices

The viscose reference was dealt with as a matter of urgency. The PIB set up a team chaired by one of its officials with a secretary who was allocated full-time to these inquiries (and who subsequently joined Courtaulds). The PIB member responsible for the inquiry was Mr S Mortimer. Courtaulds set up a team of three to deal with the PIB.

Courtaulds had notified the Board of Trade in the autumn of 1968 that a substantial increase might be needed in the price of viscose yarns, and wrote formally on 9 December 1968 under the Early Warning System giving four weeks' notice of their intention to increase prices by 6d a pound. Charges for the processing of viscose yarns had been increased, but were also covered by the reference. The case for an increase in yarn prices was based on the losses being incurred. Further cost increases were foreseen. Continuing losses would hasten the shutting down of factories in areas where there was little other activity. There had been a fall in home sales and more was being sold in export markets at low prices.

A preliminary meeting was held on 28 February and it was agreed that Courtaulds would send a paper. The paper, dated 18 March 1969, indicated that the proposed price increase might make it possible to earn a pre-tax return of 10 per cent on written-down capital employed of £6M in one part of the business and $5\frac{1}{2}$ per cent on £4M in another part. This provoked some detailed questions from Mr Mortimer with the suggestion that there should be discussions between the two staffs, to which the Chairman replied on 28 March and offered a further meeting between the two of them. This took place on 1 April and Mr (now Professor) W B Reddaway was among those present.

The PIB people said that they could not support an across-the-board increase of 6d behind the relatively high tariff, but asked for a 'forward-looking' document dealing with re-structuring the prices and necessary redundancies. Draft documents, dated 22 and 23 April, were prepared to deal with the PIB questions and were discussed with PIB staff at a meeting on 24 April and sent to Mr Mortimer on 28 April. A further meeting with him took place on 1 May and interest was displayed in the cost factors lying behind the processing charge increases already made in December 1968. Further exchanges took place and a draft report (leaving out conclusions) was shown on 30 May.

The report noted that the proposed increase of 6d would have represented an average of 9 per cent, that Courtaulds had subsequently reduced their product range, and that after consultation the prices had been restructured to give an increase of 5 per cent.

Acetate prices

Courtaulds were not even seeking to increase acetate prices. The small producer Lansil had wanted an increase but withdrew, so the PIB report had to be based on the White Paper (Cmnd 3590) provisions that prices should be reduced in certain circumstances. The acetate situation was particularly affected by the oil surcharge of 2d a gallon imposed in July 1967 which raised acetate costs. A price surcharge was imposed and shown separately on invoices. The Board of Trade noted that the surcharge would be withdrawn when the oil surcharge was removed and wrote asking Courtaulds' intentions when the oil surcharge was reduced in July 1968. Discussions and correspondence continued until December, during which Courtaulds drew attention to other cost increases far exceeding the effect of the oil surcharge reduction. This was unacceptable to the Board because it was 'tantamount to our agreeing to an increase in prices in circumstances in which we had no opportunity of considering whether the proposed increase satisfies the criteria . . .'

The PIB investigation followed much the same line as that for viscose yarns, with detailed inquiry into costs, prices and profits. The report published in October 1969 recommended that prices should be reduced immediately by $\frac{3}{4}$d a pound, and that Whitehall should keep acetate prices under review in future.

The chief reason for the proposed immediate price reduction was that labour productivity in acetate had risen faster than the national average, without any compensating increases in other costs. This had resulted in a rising trend in acetate profits, with the benefit of higher productivity not being passed on to the consumer. Courtaulds, it was said, had been able to achieve this result because of its monopoly position and tariff protection. Under these conditions the criteria of the White Paper on Prices and Incomes called for a price reduction. The actual reduction recommended was $\frac{3}{4}$d a pound, which was the balance of the oil surcharge originally added to yarn prices in 1967.

The statement that acetate yarn profits have been rising was simply untrue. The PIB had been shown an extract from a

Courtaulds' Board paper, as shown in the table. Courtaulds also indicated that yarn profits were over 25 per cent down so far in 1969–70, implying an annual rate of £4½M, which was lower than every other year since 1966–67. The PIB rejected the above evidence (see para 33[2]) on the grounds that the

UK acetate profits
(£'000)

Sales to	1968–69	1967–68	1966–67	1965–66	1964–65
Yarns	5 710	4 620	3 580	5 140	4 670
Chemicals	3 200	2 460	2 380	2 570	2 100
Plastics	1 520	1 260	630	700	670

profits of the three activities could not be ascertained separately. While it is true that the absolute amounts of profit attributed to each activity depends on arbitrary transfer prices and the allocation of joint costs, these difficulties did not affect the trend of relative profitability over a number of years, since common conventions had been used throughout. How could the PIB possibly have concluded on the evidence that over this period yarn profits increased?

The figures of productivity improvements related to process labour in spinning, solvent recovery, and dope preparation. While the productivity of process labour is an important though crude indicator of operating efficiency, it represents only about 10 per cent of costs. None-the-less the PIB seem to have based their entire case for a price reduction on this alone, ignoring the many other and complex factors affecting productivity (such as denier mix, product mix, package, raw material usage, quality). In any case the large increases (10 per cent per annum) up to 1965 were the result of enormous managerial and technical efforts devoted to help make acetate viable after the merger with British Celanese (who had virtually written off acetate as a bad job); the improvement achieved merely restored profitability to a tolerable level. The increase of 20 per cent from 1965–66 to 1968–69 was not much different from that of manufacturing industry as a whole, and was virtually all absorbed in wage increases.

[2] *Man-made Fibre and Cotton Yarn Prices* (Second Report) October 1969.

In short, it seemed to Courtaulds that neither the 'change in profits' argument, nor the 'productivity' argument used by the PIB to support a price reduction had any foundation in fact.

Both the flimsiness of these arguments and the PIB's recommendation that acetate profits be kept under review suggest that the PIB believed that Courtaulds were either abusing monopoly power already, or might do so in the future; but home prices were lower than the landed prices Courtaulds could sell at in foreign producers' countries (see para 34 of report and attachment). These figures were based on actual export performances so the problem of list prices and hidden discounts did not apply. Figures of consumption of acetate per head in various Western countries showed that, far from charging high prices and restricting output, Courtaulds had developed the UK market to a greater degree than any other European country and charged lower prices.

Quite apart from this powerful evidence (which the PIB chose to ignore) that Courtaulds were not exploiting their position, it is hard to see how they could have been allowed to by the strength of competition. First Lansil was already established in the UK markets. It is owned by a US company (Monsanto) with greater financial resources than Courtaulds and all the requisite technical know-how; it could easily have expanded if it had been profitable to do so (Monsanto was expanding nylon and acrylic production). Secondly, the process is long-established and free from patent protection. Thirdly, there are plenty of world acetate producers. Finally, acetate is only one of a number of closely competing substitutes, and margins will be subjected to increasing pressure from the growth of synthetic fibres whose costs will be falling while acetate costs will be rising.

The PIB seemed to be taking the view that regardless of the company's efficiency and expansionary policies, they should not be allowed to earn more than some given preconceived return on capital. But what does this mean in practice? First, what figure should be chosen? The Monopolies Commission did not object to returns on historic cost of over 50 per cent in the case of Cigarette Components and 20 per cent and 33 per cent for Pilkington and Triplex. These figures compared with a 'high' of 28 per cent for British Celanese on fibres and chemicals in a boom year, and a typical return over recent years of 20 per cent (as earned in the first half of 1969–70). Why was British Celanese under suspicion? Secondly, how did the PIB take account of such factors as risk, variability of profits, the different age of plant, and the effect of inflation (all of which can legitimately be considered important factors)? Thirdly, and perhaps most important, any arbitrary limit on the return on capital regarded as acceptable takes away any motive for increasing efficiency above the critical point. For example, Courtaulds had spent a good deal of effort creating exports for Tricel, particularly in Germany, and this contributed significantly to the good profit performance in 1968–1969. If home prices had to be adjusted to restrict overall return to, say, 25 per cent, such efforts would simply be self-defeating, and the company would inevitably be led to switch managerial and financial resources elsewhere.

The PIB's case for both a price reduction and for a continuing review seemed groundless. Courtaulds had recently co-operated in enquiries from the Monopolies Commission, the Board of Trade (tariff inquiry) and the PIB, and they believed they had produced enough evidence to convince any unprejudiced observer that on the whole they were efficient; they were innovators; their prices were low; and their export performance was excellent. They accepted that monopolists need to be subject to periodical review, but continuous interference could only divert management from the more important task of running the business.

The situation led to an internal enquiry in January 1970 as to the powers, if any, for enforcing the PIB recommendation. It appeared that there was no compulsory power which would enable a government department, or anyone else, to compel Courtaulds to comply. If the Board recommended a reduction of a price, the Minister could only enforce it if in his original reference he had requested the Prices and Incomes Board to make a recommendation; but there was no such request. The requirement that the reference must call for a recommendation is contained in section 4(1) of the Prices and Incomes Act 1968. Accordingly, if the Minister wished to insist on the reduction he would have had to re-refer the matter to the Board, but on this occasion asking for a recommendation. A whole new inquiry would have to be set on foot.

Management also wished to know whether they were entitled in law to increase the price of acetate yarn. No Order had been made under section 7 of the Prices and Incomes Act 1966 applying to prices of yarn, and there appeared to be no compulsion upon Courtaulds not to increase the price. However, the Minister could of course make a reference if the price was increased.

In January the Ministry of Technology were told of Courtaulds' intention to rationalise the acetate yarn price list in minor ways which would increase revenues by £60 000, but a probable switch between products could effectively reduce average prices realised by £20 000. Increases since April–May 1969 when the PIB investigated had added £465 000 to costs. By June, cost increases for materials were running at an annual rate of £730 000. After some adjustments in April, price increases were eventually implemented from July on all acetate yarns. The Ministry of Technology confirmed that no objection was to be raised, either on these, or on viscose staple or tyre yarn price increases announced at the same time.

REFLECTIONS ON THE INQUIRIES

Intellectual attitudes
The Monopolies Commission inquiry, as the most exhaustive, prolonged, and damaging to the company, naturally provokes the most thought. It was difficult from outside to understand the reasons which led to the reference. The President soothingly implied that it was a necessary use of the machinery set up under the Act and it just happened to be Courtaulds' turn to come up for consideration. It has been suggested that the reference was a response to the acquisitions and expansion described in Chapter 3. But neither of these explanations is consistent with the limitation of the reference to the cellulosic fibres. The first should surely have led to a reference of all man-made fibres; the second to a reference of the man-made fibre industry together with the appropriate fibre-using industries.

F

The government had no powers to refer Courtaulds as such to the Commission.

More likely is it that ambivalent attitudes prevailed in the Board of Trade. On the one hand Courtaulds may have been seen as a power for good in a seemingly depressed industry; on the other hand the large number and scale of their merger activities and the increase in concentration that resulted gave rise to monopoly considerations. To investigate the whole field would be enormously costly, time consuming and disruptive, so why not compromise; investigate a major part of the Courtaulds business in depth, see what the Commission discovers, and refer other parts later if that seemed justified? Close examination of a part would give significant insights into the whole. With two Divisions concerned in the Board of Trade—that responsible for the textile industry, and that responsible for the monopoly policy and its administration—the compromise solution is a plausible hypothesis.

But it ignored the reality of Courtaulds as a single business specialising in textiles, led by the Chairman and a group of executives whose concern was the total enterprise. Decisions about part of its textile business have to be judged in relation to the whole, so that the balance of understanding of the Monopolies Commission was almost certain to be faulty. In a fully diversified business, to examine one part which is separable from the rest may not give rise to these distortions, but to examine part of a part is inviting trouble.

There was another major stumbling block in the way of a proper understanding of Courtaulds' business. A White Paper on Productivity, Prices and Incomes published in December 1969 was followed by a consultative document from the DEP in January and a Bill in March which might have led to the merging of the Monopolies Commission and the PIB.

Although these changes never became effective, the December 1969 White Paper contains a significant pointer to Whitehall attitudes:

. . . it is increasingly difficult to rely on traditional market forces alone to protect consumers. Indeed, there are many parts of the economy where conditions of even near perfect competition do not exist. In this situation continuing viligance over prices is needed.

The concept of perfect competition looms large in academic thinking and has influenced official thinking on the public interest in relation to industry. It may have been responsible for much of the failure of understanding which appeared in the Monopolies Commission report; and if so it contributed to the feelings of anger and frustration on the Courtaulds side which affected relations with Whitehall for some while afterwards. It is necessary for the purpose of this study, therefore, to examine this concept in more detail and the ways in which it is inappropriate to the understanding of industrial activity which must be a necessary preliminary to effective prescription. This is done in Chapter 9.

Defects of procedure
In the Courtaulds case the issues involved were formulated only at a late stage in the proceedings, by which time the company was handicapped in presenting a full and balanced statement of relevant circumstances.

Evidence, often hostile to Courtaulds, was given by other persons in the absence of representatives of the company. Nor was the evidence subsequently put to the company, except sometimes in a highly abbreviated form. Hence it was difficult, if not impossible, to challenge the accuracy of any adverse allegation. Moreover, even where there was the opportunity to comment in writing on this abbreviated form of the allegation, those comments were not referred back to the party making the allegation. Evidence did not seem to be sufficiently challenged and tested by the Commission, and the value and accuracy of their report suffered as a result. Sometimes the Commission did not even attempt to resolve a conflict of evidence; both views were recorded, one often in a footnote, thus leaving the reader with the impression that for some reason, not apparent from the report, the Commission preferred that in the main text.

The Secretariat of the Commission, who are largely the evidence-seeking body and who presented the case to the

Commission, seemed too closely connected with the Commission itself and lacked a sufficient number of professionally qualified people, in particular accountants, lawyers and economists.

Only certain factual parts of the report were seen by the company before publication. The company did not know until the date of publication either the Commission's findings or its recommendations. The Commission did not put its proposed recommendations to the company and therefore made them without fully considering their likely practical effects.

These procedural defects could be remedied.

The task of presenting a case to the Commission could cease to be undertaken by the Secretariat of the Commission, and instead should become the task of an entirely separate department along the lines of that of the Registrar of Restrictive Trade Practices, possibly (to avoid the need for legislation) set up as the research department of a reformed Monopolies Commission. The new department should be provided with a strong staff, including technologists, accountants, lawyers and economists. In seeking factual evidence, the investigators should disclose not only the information required but also the purposes for which it is wanted. All written evidence should be submitted to those being investigated who should have the right to call for opponents to attend for cross-examination.

As soon as the investigators are satisfied that they have all the evidence they need, they should formulate the precise issues raised by the evidence in relation to the public interest. Copies of the case which it is proposed to present should then be sent to those under investigation. At this stage the Commission is not committed to anything more than the responsibility for making the investigators' report available for comment.

Before it is submitted to the Minister, the report of the Commission should be submitted in draft to the company under investigation. They should then be entitled to try to persuade the Commission orally or in writing to modify the report. At this point, the Commission would be able to examine more thoroughly the practical effect of any recommendations proposed to be made. If the Commission was unwilling to adopt any modification proposed by the company, and the company had submitted written comments of a reasonable length, it should be the duty of the Commission to incorporate those comments in an appendix which should form part of the published report.

Such changes would go a long way towards removing some of the feelings of injustice to which the Courtaulds proceedings gave rise.

Comparisons between the Commission and the PIB
Generally in dealings with the PIB, however irritating and misconceived some of their conclusions might be, as compared with the Monopolies Commission there was a refreshing willingness on their part—both members and senior officials—to engage in direct across-the-table discussion of the real issues, to confine their enquiries to those issues and to move with commendable speed. There was a curious inclination to want to treat each product as if it stood on its own and a consequent reluctance to admit that cash flows are employed in relation to a company's assessment of its future possibilities and without reference to where they have emerged. This looks like a by-product of the economists' one-product firm model and the conclusions derived from it, and suggests that the PIB—like the Commission—had no model for dealing with the multi-product firm as a portfolio of risk-situations consisting in products at different stages in their life-cycles and with varying cash flow contributions or needs.

However, the PIB, unlike the Commission, had a first-class team of highly qualified research workers. Their working methods encouraged direct dealings and enabled the two sides to achieve a degree of mutual respect and agreement on the issues which needed further study. The employment of outside consultants of outstanding calibre enabled the PIB to supplement the work of its own staff, and by bringing the consultants into the direct confrontations, ensured that their intellectual contribution was not muffled.

The PIB technique of appointing one Board member to take charge of each enquiry and to deal with the company means that the results of the various interchanges were well co-ordinated. It was obvious from the company's side that there was a rapid appraisal of information received in the PIB office through whatever channels, and therefore a sense of a live continuing relationship—almost a negotiation.

The extent to which these differences derived from the differing personalities and backgrounds of the two chairmen must be a matter of speculation. But it would be easy to understand that the PIB methods would come more naturally to a politician-cum-businessman than to a professional lawyer.

Of course the PIB had some fairly precise guidelines against which to judge the situations referred to it, whereas the Commission had to deal with the much vaguer concept of the public interest. It would surely be possible, however, for a reformed Commission with a suitable research staff to formulate some guidelines as to how it would judge the public interest, perhaps even for the staff's ideas to be the subject of public hearings and debate, leading to a report which, once accepted by the Minister, could guide the Commission and those liable to be referred to it in the future. This would leave open the possibility of further discussion and debate and new guidelines as experience accumulated.

In this respect the methods adopted by the Commission on the Third London Airport may be worth studying. The research team's analysis and assessment of all the circumstances relating to the four short-listed sites was made available to anyone who had an interest, and without in any way committing the Commission. It provided the basis for debate and an extensive series of public hearings, all of which influenced the final report. A similar attempt to arrive at a statement of where the public interest resides in relation to a particular industry and to the market power possessed by the firms concerned should help to make generally acceptable judgements on individual cases, and thus to an improved understanding between government and industry in one necessary area of common action.

Conflicting signals

Market power can be misused, and there must be suitable arrangements for safeguarding the public interest. But it can be asked whether it was sensible in the case under study to initiate the extensive inquiries described in this chapter at the same time as the company—with government support—was so deeply and with such difficulty involved in the activities described in the previous chapter. To undertake a programme of modernisation and structural change on the scale which was required in Lancashire was not embarked upon for altruistic reasons: it was necessary to the company's survival. But it did offer a prospect of dealing with a problem which governments had found intractable, and this was recognised in various ways, including some of the public ministerial statements quoted in Chapter 5.

A greater understanding of the total situation might have led to a more wholehearted support for what the company was doing, with the deferment of any investigation for a period of some years. The feelings of frustration which have been referred to were only in part caused by the Commission's (and to a lesser extent the PIB's) failures of understanding and imperfect procedures. They were just as much the result of feeling that what government was encouraging with one hand it was seeking to discourage with the other. A company is a small group with limited capacity and energies if one is concerned, as here, with high level strategy and overall direction. Government with its multiplicity of agencies and the variety of interests with which it is concerned can impinge adversely on the behaviour of that small group, through seeking to do too many things at once and not recognising that the management processes of business need to be vastly different from those of bureaucracy.

It is also irrelevant from management's point of view that some topics involved dealing with civil servants and others with external agencies. All, so far as management is concerned, form part of the Whitehall machine and in pursuing their investigatory functions are diverting a few senior people away from their primary and demanding task. It is equally irrelevant that the agencies have different functions: their effect on the business impinges on the same few individuals.

CARBON FIBRES

This chapter has been concerned with major interventions in the company's affairs which were of far-reaching importance. To illustrate the variety of what goes on it may be useful to conclude with an episode of quite a different type.

Courtaulds believed that carbon fibres have a future and spent money on developing the precursor and their own route to discontinuous and continuous lengths of fibre. Total production by 1968 was about one ton a month; the chief producer being Rolls Royce, the second Courtaulds.

On 21 November 1968 Courtaulds were notified by the Secretary to the Sub-Committee of the Parliamentary Select Committee, Science and Technology, that they would be required to give evidence on 4 December. The session would be in private but the evidence would be published. Courtaulds were invited to submit a preliminary memorandum about their work on carbon fibres. The parliamentary interest had its roots to a certain extent in an article by David Fishlock in the *Financial Times* of 18 July which had indicated a slow rate of development and suggested that a plant to make tens of tons a year ought to be built. On 3 December 1968 Fishlock wrote a further article which put the matter in better perspective but the parliamentary reaction had already been over-enthusiastic. Courtaulds submitted a memorandum on 29 November and Mr Mathys, Mr Entwistle and Dr Vera Furness, the Director of Research, gave evidence on 4 December for one hour to four MPs. The report was published on 14 March 1969, calling for a large-scale plant to produce 450 tons a year at a cost of £5 M as being of the utmost national importance.

There was considerable press comment. On 26 March the Chairman replied to a letter from Wedgwood Benn placing the development in perspective and saying that the Sub-Committee appeared totally to have ignored the Courtaulds evidence. It was clear that the Ministry of Technology was put on the spot by the Report and this was underlined in articles in *The Times* on 27 May 1969. ICI was reported to be undertaking a major market survey in June and there was parliamentary pressure on Wedgwood Benn from July to December to declare the government's intention for supporting this technology. Brian Parkyn, the Chairman of the Sub-Committee, was obviously pressing the government by building this up into a *cause célèbre* to see how far Britain was prepared to pursue a technology in order to get a commercial pay-off. In March 1970 Courtaulds were invited to supply a second memorandum updating their evidence. The summer General Election brought the parliamentary interest to a close. ICI decided to do nothing.

The carbon fibre episode is an illustration of the way in which parliamentary interest can be aroused in a specific example of a topic of general public concern (in this case whether private industry needed prodding properly to exploit new technology). As a result of that parliamentary interest government feels induced to consider action. And the final result is that, though nobody would admit it, the activities and plans of the industrialists concerned are seen to be adequate to the situation. Though no general conclusion can be drawn that the activities and plans of industrialists are always adequate to the needs of the situation, the carbon fibre story supplies a cautionary tale for those who are inclined always to believe the converse.

Chapter Seven

GOVERNMENT—RESPONSE TO GENERAL POLICIES

Whilst the two preceding chapters have examined government policies and actions which related specifically to the textile industry and to Courtaulds, this chapter is concerned with the company's response to those policies of more general and uniform application to all industry.

The field of interest here is vast, and extends to regional policies, investment incentives, taxation policy in all its aspects, the response to the general market conditions created by EFTA and prospective entry into EEC, industrial relations, education and training, safety and the protection of the environment and legislation about restrictive practices. Some process of selection is therefore inevitable, even though it diminishes the comprehensiveness of this attempt to study in the case of one firm all aspects of the government–industry relationship.

Regional policy and investment incentives appear to be the areas in which government policies have had the greatest influence, and there has been a close interconnection between them. Of the £182M invested by the Group in the five years to March 1970, £40M was provided from incentives, the major part of which came from additional incentives provided for setting up in development and special development areas.

In selecting these two issues for more detailed consideration later in this chapter, it is important to stress the extent to which the picture of government–industry relationships—as exemplified in the Courtaulds case—is being distorted in a number of ways. Omission alone can distort even where the relationship neither gives rise to a major continuing administrative interchange nor to any significant effect on the way the firm runs or the results it achieves.

Thus the Restrictive Trade Practices Act led to a review of agreements and arrangements, some changes in them, some policy guidance and a growing general understanding throughout the organisation of its implications. The Industrial Training Act had no important effects because training arrangements were fairly well developed and the formal existence of a Board made little difference. In the industrial relations field there were isolated situations in which the firm's activities became involved with those of government, but generally the firm's dealings with its employees and with their unions have been based on freely negotiated arrangements in conditions to which the minimum standards imposed by law have not been applicable.

One exception occurred in 1966 when some ladies in Stockport, where a factory was being closed, protested to their MP because their colleagues were to receive redundancy pay whereas they had been offered alternative employment so that, as the company interpreted the Redundancy Payments Act, they disqualified themselves from entitlement to redundancy pay once they refused that alternative employment; and this led to a hearing before the Manchester Industrial Tribunal which made an award against the company. Another exceptional situation arose in the industrial relations field when in 1971 members of ASTMS employed at the Spennymoor plant in Durham struck because of the alleged wrongful dismissal of one of their number; and an inquiry instituted under the Conciliation Act 1896 found that he had not been victimised, though criticisms were made of both company and union.

In other areas the government–industry relationship may give rise to considerable administrative work without there being any important effect on the business, and this has probably been the case so far as Courtaulds is concerned with purchase tax and SET; both have given rise to irritating and time-consuming exchanges with government in dealing with borderline cases.

Taxation generally represents a third area where there is both a considerable administrative load and the possibility of a substantial effect on the company's results, if not on the way the business is run (though investment incentives call for special discussion below). In dealing with tax, Lord Clyde's dictum prevails:

> No man in this country is under the smallest obligation, moral or other, so to arrange his legal arrangements to his business or to his property as to enable the Inland Revenue to put the largest possible shovel into his stores. The Inland Revenue is not slow—and quite rightly—to take every advantage which is open to it under the taxing statutes for the purpose of depleting the taxpayer's pocket. And the taxpayer is in like manner entitled to be astute to prevent, so far as he honestly can, the depletion of his means by the Revenue.[1]

THE ROLE OF THE CBI

In managing government business specific to the company, the normal practice would be for direct dealings between the company and the departments concerned, although there may be exceptions where the issue is of wider concern—the Lancashire problem, for example. In dealing with the general issues considered in this chapter, however, there is a more obvious choice to be made between direct representation to the government and participation in the work of the appropriate representative body, usually the CBI. In formulating views about the EEC, for example, there was never any doubt that the CBI was a most effective channel, because its predecessor (the FBI) had established itself at an early stage in the debate as giving a lead which the company accepted (after some initial hesitancy).

Similarly, in general taxation matters the company has looked to the CBI Taxation Panel as the main instrument for formulating and expressing views, though with a less wholehearted conviction. There has at times been a preoccupation with estate duty, capital gains tax and similar issues which seemed secondary to the interests of the larger members; on one occasion drafting of the CBI's budget representations had

---

[1] Ayrshire Pullman Motor Services & Ritchie *v.* IRC (1929), 14 Tax Cases 754 per The Lord President of the Court of Session.

reached an advanced stage without reference to the desirability of a reduction in corporation tax, realistic in the circumstances and in fact included in the Chancellor's budget proposals.

A recently formed confederation of many thousands of firms might be inclined to underestimate the importance of stressing the claims of the 400 companies which between them account for some 80 per cent of UK manufacturing industry. The formation in 1967 of the Industrial Policy Group (in which Courtaulds played no part and does not participate) provides a means for reflecting the interests of the bigger concerns, though so far it has confined itself to general background research papers on subjects relevant to big company interests. The CBI sometimes finds it difficult to reconcile the interests of the big companies, as in its representations in 1972 about the proposed changes in the corporation tax system where, faced by the parliamentary Select Committee with a question about choosing between the interests of companies with primarily overseas earnings and those with primarily UK earnings, the chairman of the CBI Taxation Panel and the CBI official appeared in their answers to lean towards the interests of those with overseas earnings! And when it was decided that investment grants would be paid only in respect of contracts entered into before October 1970 and the Department of Trade and Industry appeared to be placing too narrow an interpretation on when a contract could be said to exist, Courtaulds decided to make their own representations direct to the Minister, keeping the CBI informed; and in this they were influenced by the knowledge that two other large companies, similarly affected, hoped to have protected their interests in other ways which were not thought by Courtaulds to be particularly likely to succeed, though they would make it more difficult than usual to ensure a clear directive to the CBI staff.

ISSUES OF REGIONAL AND EMPLOYMENT POLICY

Northern Ireland
Work on the first factory at Carrickfergus began in July 1946 and production started in June 1950. At that time capital grants

and other incentives did not exist in Northern Ireland. The availability of suitable workers was an important factor. By the time capital grant assistance was introduced in 1954 a major part of the project was completed. Even then claims were not made until the financial year 1956–57 because, it was argued, acceptance of grants might place the company under an undesirable moral obligation to the Northern Ireland government and lead to interference in some circumstances. It was noted in April 1957 that officials 'are astonished at the company's refusal of substantial sums of money in the past.'

Such inhibitions did not appear subsequently, and the combination of available workers and financial help appeared to make Northern Ireland an attractive area for some of the internally generated expansion in the fibre-using activities following 1962. The acquisition of a majority shareholding in Crepe Weavers in 1965, and of Moygashel in 1968, both primarily Ulster-based companies, further extended the company's stake in the Province, until the numbers employed there had made Courtaulds second only to Harland & Wolff as employers—though more widely dispersed—and accounted for about 10 per cent of the Group's employment in the UK.

Great Britain

The pre-war legislation of 1934, 1936 and 1937, following the depression of the 1930s, had no important influence on the company's development; but the 1945 Act and subsequent legislation[2] was a major influence, first because of the administrative work involved in seeking permission to build or extend, and second because of the financial incentives to invest in some areas rather than others.

The administrative load increased in part as a result of changes in type of production unit. The Group shifted the balance of its investment away from dependence on a relatively few large capital-intensive sites each employing 2000 persons or more, and towards its fibre-using activities, which were more dispersed, with fewer numbers on each site and with a

[2] 1947 Town and Country Planning Act; Local Employment Acts 1960 and 1963, 1966 Industrial Development Act.

higher proportion of women. From July 1967 until October 1971 there were forty-two applications for Industrial Development Certificates (IDCs) in non-development areas, relating in all to about 1.5 million square feet of factory space and some 3000 workers.

The Industrial Development Act 1966 was most significant, having regard to the timing of Courtaulds' own expansions. Its provisions were encouraging—40 per cent grants towards machinery expenditure in development areas as compared with 20 per cent elsewhere; loans and training grants. And the Special Development Area arrangements announced in November 1967 gave additional incentives. The further measures introduced after 1970 by the Conservative government came too late to affect the major expansion plans outlined in Chapter 3, which by then were virtually committed: indeed, expenditure was tailing off.

The major projects encouraged by these incentives were the weaving mills at Carlisle, Lillyhall and Skelmersdale and the worsted spinning unit at Spennymoor in Durham employing former miners. The weaving mills were well away from the traditional Lancashire weaving areas and provoked some adverse public comment in consequence. Skelmersdale, as a new town populated largely from Liverpool dock areas, gave rise to special training and industrial relations problems. But without the financial incentives these large projects may not have gone ahead, and certainly would not have been located in these areas.

Negotiations concerning Industrial Development Certificates
An example will give a general impression of how location decisions were handled. In the autumn of 1967, applications for Industrial Development Certificates had been submitted by four group knitting companies in the East Midlands. There were already others under consideration. Board of Trade officials were unhappy about this piecemeal presentation. It would have suited them to have an overall picture of projected expansions over perhaps a two-year period; but in particular they sought a presentation of the balance between the company's projected expansions in Development Areas, and those

projects which were more politically difficult to accommodate under the regional policies.

There followed a series of informal discussions in which a 'package deal' was considered, Courtaulds having at the time plans to expand in nylon yarn processing and warp knitting at Aintree, as well as possibly further worsted spinning development in Cumberland and some garment making in Newcastle. The projected Lillyhall weaving project was also something to set against the half dozen or so 'difficult' applications. However, it was not feasible to reach any kind of fixed agreement because of the Group's diversity and rate of growth. For example, within a fortnight between two discussions with officials two further possible projects had presented themselves, one in and one outside a Development Area. It was necessary to keep officials informed on a continuing basis so that the Group's contribution to regional development policy might be assessed at any time, and for this the company's head office staff was notified of all expansion projects and kept up a running dialogue with officials in Distribution of Industry Division. Courtaulds had been the first company to go to a Special Development Area, with the worsted spinning project at Spennymoor, and this helped in the discussions with officials.

Plant closures

With the reorganisation of company plants, particularly in Lancashire, a number of them had to be closed. These were normally dealt with through consultation between management, union officials and the local offices of the Department of Employment and Productivity. However, the difficulties of the viscose filament yarn business (already referred to in discussing the PIB reference) made it necessary finally to shut the Wolverhampton factory and, since this gave rise to a short parliamentary debate, it deserves mention here.

In 1966 Courtaulds announced a streamlining operation at Wolverhampton to improve productivity. Out of a total 1600 employees it was expected that there would be not more than forty redundancies, the rest transferring elsewhere. In fact about 120 to 150 in total were affected. In May 1970

Courtaulds announced that, despite strenuous efforts to make improvements, the losses in viscose operations at Wolverhampton had continued and therefore they planned a phased closure. Courtaulds went through the normal procedure of informing the Production Division in the Ministry of Technology (which had taken over the functions previously exercised by the Board of Trade). Already on 20 May there had been a call from a member of the Division asking about the implications of running down textile yarn production, the implicit reason for the inquiry being import substitution questions and potential duty remission or section 7 applications, although this was not stated. Courtaulds explained that substitutes and comparable yarns were available from other factories. The Department of Employment and Productivity had been in touch for background information at the suggestion of the Ministry of Technology and were told that 1300 people would be involved at Wolverhampton.

On 21 May explanatory letters were sent by Courtaulds to the MPs concerned, Mrs Renée Short and Mr Enoch Powell. An angry letter from Mrs Short was followed on 3 July by a meeting with her. Just after this meeting a change of plan was announced which meant immediate closure instead of gradual phasing, since it had been impossible to work the running down as planned because of union insistence on operation of the principle of 'last in first out.' Following a parliamentary question of 16 July, Mrs Short raised the matter in a half-hour adjournment debate on 22 July referring to ruthless capitalism, transferring abroad of production as being the sign of worse to come and of Courtaulds throwing 1300 people on the 'scrap heap.'

Courtaulds' position was defended by a Member of Parliament with a constituency interest, who had sought information prior to the debate because he wanted to establish the facts. Mr Nicholas Ridley, Parliamentary Secretary at the Ministry of Technology, who took the debate, dealt with the allegation about excessive profits by saying that the Group's total pre-tax profit of £52M represented only 11.4 per cent return on capital. He referred to the generosity of the company in giving more than the minimum redundancy payments and benefits, and *ex gratia* payments to some employees, and attempted to tone down the hysteria by pointing out that the Wolverhampton unemployment rate was only 2.1 per cent and that there was a good chance of redeployment. The matter was again raised by Mrs Short on 21 July 1970 in the debate on the EEC White Paper, when she said that Courtaulds' action in Wolverhampton had 'clinched' her opposition to 'economic policies pursued by the Six.' Her assertions were questioned in a letter on 22 July.

INVESTMENT GRANTS

The history of investment incentive betrays a government obsession with achieving quick results. This bears little relation to the time-scale within which major investment plans are conceived and carried through, and some of the changes showed little appreciation that the largest firms account for most of the new investment in manufacturing industry.

By 1964, according to the Report of the Committee on Turnover Tax (Cmnd 2300 March 1964), investment incentives to UK industry were at least as generous as those available to industry in other developed countries, and usually more so. These incentives, provided through tax remissions, were well understood by those who made use of them. The extended use of discounted cash flow techniques for investment appraisal was making it easier for all to see their implications for individual decisions, and indeed in 1965 the National Economic Development Office published a booklet giving a simple exposition of these appraisal methods.

However, low investment in UK industry by international standards was a major preoccupation of government. In his budget speech in 1965 the Chancellor (Mr J Callaghan) undertook to review the system. The CBI sent a questionnaire to all and sundry, ignoring the concentration of spending. The results three months later showed no decisive weight of opinion. It was decided to press the case for free depreciation which was unlikely to be politically acceptable at that time. In the public discussion the view was expressed that the prevailing system was too complicated. This view appears to have been much influenced by a study[3] made in a limited section of the engineering industry relating to a sector of investment representing under 10 per cent of total fixed capital expenditure in manufacturing industry.

A grant system was introduced. The new system transferred responsibility to the Board of Trade and required the employment of 2000 officials and imposed new administrative burdens within companies. The earlier system had been dealt with as a part of the Inland Revenue's annual tax assessment procedures.

However, when by 1970 there was a Conservative government and a prospect of further change, Courtaulds argued for retaining the grants system—continuity being more important in this field than theoretical arguments. But changes were made and the transition from the grants system brought its own painful problems.

A properly established system for appraising investment projects can adapt to changing rules of the game, but not without cost and inconvenience. What is more difficult to adapt is the firm's investment strategy. Lines of development which look good under one system look less good under another system; a strategy which takes full account of tax payments has widespread implications, and a change in the tax system has widespread effects. But they can come about only slowly, for commitments have been entered into, an interconnected series of investment decisions embarked upon, employees have been prepared for future changes, and so on. And a differently calculated financial prospect arising from an investment may only in a few cases cause a specific decision to be different, for the financial appraisal is only part of the process of making an investment decision.

A COMMENT

Regional policy and investment incentives were selected for examination because, of all the general policies to which the company has responded, they have had the greatest influence on what has happened. The evidence given in this chapter does

[3] R R Neild, *Replacement Policy* (*National Institute Economic Review*, November 1964).

indeed confirm their effectiveness. Yet as examples of the industry–government relationship these areas of policy have not given rise to the controversies, and thus to the diversion of senior management effort, which have characterised the more selective and, from the company's viewpoint, less effective interventions. It is interesting—and germane to the theme—to speculate on the reasons for this.

It must surely be pertinent that in regional and investment policies, government objectives were clear, capable of being expressed in decisions which had a precise meaning to both the officials and those in industry and of being implemented without any feeling that the mainsprings of successful business behaviour were being attacked. Nevertheless this has not been because these two general policies have any less significant relation to the public interest than those which gave rise to the selective interventions. As said in the NEDO publication on Investment Appraisal,

> In considering the rationality of investment decisions, the problem has to be faced that the decision most favourable to the private firm may not always be most beneficial to the community. It is assumed here, however, that fiscal and other policies are operated so as to ensure that social and private net returns from investment are kept fairly well in line.

Even though the systems of regional policy and investment incentives underwent a number of changes over the years, the interpretation and indications of what degree of flexibility might be possible have always been clear, bar a few administrative wranglings.

Chapter Eight

GOVERNMENT—THE EFFECTS ON COURTAULDS

To assess effects within such a short time of the events is hazardous, especially in relation to an institution which has had a continuity of development over some 170 years, where the career time-span of the individuals most affected is at least twenty years and where the key positions are held for a period of ten years or more. According to Ulton (*Industrial Concentration 1970*, p 90), of the fifty largest British manufacturing companies (ranked according to profits) before 1924, about one-fifth of them fell out of the list in each decade. By 1950 the drop-out rate in each decade had increased to two-fifths and has since remained at that level. The top is indeed a slippery place, and in looking at the Courtaulds case it is early in terms both of institutional history and of individuals' responses to form judgements.

However, judgements are essential to the task on which we are engaged, and essential also to the effort to improve performance. More detailed knowledge and understanding which only time can reveal might lead to their being modified or abandoned, but some preliminary assessment is appropriate.

REGIONAL AND INVESTMENT INCENTIVES

It is easier to feel sure about the effects of some of the more general policies applicable to all firms and industries. There is no doubt that of the 130 000 or so people employed by Courtaulds in the UK, a higher proportion are in Northern Ireland and in some of the Development Areas in Great Britain than would have been the case in the absence of limitations on industrial location in some areas, and without the positive encouragements to investment in others. How much contribution this made to the national interest is another question. From the more limited point of view of Courtaulds, the issues are first, whether the decisions to respond in these ways were the best possible ones, having regard to the information then available to management, or capable of being available; and secondly, whether subsequent developments have or should have led to a reappraisal of the original decisions.

There was a strong element of faith in some of the original decisions—that in Northern Ireland, communal difficulties would not reach such a pitch as to jeopardise continuity and efficiency of operations; that at Spennymoor, it would be possible to train former coal-workers into the delicate skills of handling textile fibres; that at Skelmersdale, former Liverpool dock workers could be trained in the skills of weaving and that they would come to accept the disciplines of normal factory life. In none of these instances have the acts of faith proved easy to bring to accomplishment, but there is nothing at present to suggest that the original appraisals were wrong from Courtaulds' point of view.

The effects of the policies described on the company's total investment, and therefore on the total number of jobs available, have also been considerable. It was indicated in Chapter 7 that about 25 per cent of the company's investment in the five years to March 1970 had come from grants. Gearing has been taken about as far as is prudent if the company is to maintain its financial standing and its ability to raise further cash for future needs. With annual interest payments of over £19M to be charged against a trading profit of just over £60M, Courtaulds is indeed a highly geared company by British standards. So if the grants had not been available, further borrowing might have proved impracticable; and at no time has the share price been at a sufficient level to justify raising funds by way of a rights issue. It can be concluded, therefore, that the total of investment would have been lower but for the official incentives.

It is not possible to establish the activities which might have been expanded less rapidly if there had been less cash available. The incentives made their contribution to each year's projected cash flow and thus year by year influenced attitudes about the scale of investment which could safely be undertaken. It would be highly artificial at this stage to attempt to recapture the attitudes which prevailed and the likely consequences of even greater financial stringency. The actual results of what was done in terms of trading profits would be no guide, for some projects—such as spun weaving— were undertaken in the knowledge that there would be cash losses for a while; indeed, that project had an important place in the strategy for dealing with Lancashire and with the fibre activities closely related to the health of that market.

GOVERNMENT AND TEXTILES

To appraise Courtaulds' responses to those government actions which related specifically to the Lancashire textile scene is peculiarly difficult; so much of what Courtaulds did was based on the hope that government policies would be modified suitably, as indeed occurred to a modest degree. This was a situation in which Courtaulds was giving a lead, and was being generally encouraged by ministers and others to keep doing so.

Courtaulds never formulated precisely what government action would be sufficient to offer a prospect of a satisfactory profit on their investments in the Lancashire section of the industry in 1964 and subsequently. A precise formulation might have been politically unwise anyway. The government had enough difficulty in achieving the transition from quotas to tariffs in respect of Commonwealth imports, and the subsequent extension in 1971 of quotas for 1972 in addition to the newly introduced tariffs was a major political drama, involving (it is said) a reference to the Cabinet.

Against this background it is difficult for those concerned in government to accept that these measures alone do not create an adequate basis of confidence, and it is unfortunate that the case by case approach—the *ad hoc* treatment of the textile industry discussed when Sir Donald MacDougall gave evidence to the Select Committee on 1 March 1972[1]— strengthens the hand of those who are wedded to the twin doctrines of expanding world trade through British adherence to the rules of international trade, and expanding the trade of the less developed countries through their textile exports. So the initial Courtaulds action in advance of a government lead has been succeeded by doubts—less destructive than those which existed in Lancashire in the past, because their competitive strength is greater and individual careers are less exclusively tied to Lancashire, but nevertheless potentially corroding.

Should Lancashire continue to be regarded as a special problem? The elimination of the duty-free entry of Commonwealth cottons removed the historical anomaly which has plagued the industry for so long. Increased capital intensiveness and the interchangeability of one textile product for another have removed other factors which might in the past have made Lancashire a special case. The growth of integration in the industry, and the increased awareness of interdependence, means that government policies will need always to consider the fibre, textile and garment scene as a whole. Courtaulds, as the one company which has consistently followed this line in its own development, has been conscious of the vulnerability which has resulted from the failure of government policy so far to identify the whole of the textile industry as a special case.

It can be held—and it has indeed been argued—that past attitudes and policies, creating competition and breeding uncertainty about the future, have been successful in stimulating Courtaulds' management into the actions it has taken, and that the company's relative success is thus a demonstration of the appropriateness of the policies which have been followed. This belief, if seriously held, would remove any prospect of the more encouraging policies which look necessary from the firm's point of view.

But it is difficult to believe that the lessons of experience can

[1] Minutes of Evidence, Trade and Industry Sub-Committee (of the Expenditure Committee) HMSO.

thus be misread. Svennilson[2] showed in 1954 that those industries which had been most progressive by any relevant test also had been most shielded from the worst of the depression of the 1930s, whilst those which had been most subjected to its buffetings were those which subsequently had been the most backward. While it is possible that these industries would have been backward even if the pre-war depression had not occurred, it is a fallacy to think that exposure to competitive pressures of any magnitude is conducive to good management, as the history of Lancashire shows; and the urge to struggle for survival usually requires some belief that success is possible. Courtaulds, with the relative and temporary strength derived from their strong cellulose fibre and film position, were able to embark on plans which would have been impossible for others, and their action—though dictated by enlightened self-interest—was judged (even by those who believe it to have been the benign result of competitive pressures) to have been useful from a wider viewpoint. It is also difficult to see that of all industries, textiles—and the UK textile industry of all others in developed countries—should be the one which almost alone needs competitive pressures to induce good management.

FIBRE PRICES AND POLICIES

The PIB studies and the decisions that resulted had no long-term effects on prices. The acetate yarn price recommendation was overtaken by events; cotton spun prices were not attacked; and viscose yarn prices, though raised less at the time than the company at first proposed, were adjusted experimentally as part of a continuing process of seeking to discover that combination (if any) of output and price which gave some prospect of viability; and the modest adjustment to the price increases which was made at the instance of the PIB had no lasting influence; it has been long since overtaken by events.

The acceptance by the government of the Monopolies Commission's recommendation about ending the agreements

[2] Ingvar Svennilson, *Growth and Stagnation in the European Economy* (United Nations Economic Commission for Europe, Geneva 1954).

with the EFTA producers had other consequences. Whilst the agreements operated, imports of viscose staple fibre increased. This could be expected over a period when intra-EFTA duties were declining until a nil duty position was reached from January 1967. When the agreements were ended in 1969 the import flow in fact stabilised and only rose again in 1971 in conditions of high demand.

	Imports from EFTA (million lb)
1964	9.0
1965	20.8
1966	18.4
1967	26.2
1968	33.5
1969	29.3
1970	33.4
1971	48.7

Imports from other sources remained throughout at negligible levels. Because of the relatively insignificant home markets of the EFTA countries, exports to them of viscose staple remained at insignificant levels over these years. Exports to other markets were substantial and increasing. As a proportion of the total, shipments to the EFTA countries have halved to just over 3 per cent in 1971.

The share of the UK domestic market taken by imports increased from 10.6 per cent in 1965 to 22 per cent in 1971.

The effect on profits of these changes in domestic sales volume cannot be separated from the effect of all the other factors which have been operating—cost changes, depressed UK market conditions and increased exports. Nevertheless, it is significant that in the four years to March 1971, profits from staple fibre were about 50 per cent of those in the previous four years studied by the Commission; and in the last two years of the later period they were one-third of those in the first two years of that period.

During recent years some producers overseas have abandoned production of rayon staple completely. In Holland AKZO (then AKU) abandoned staple production in 1967. In

Germany the closure of the Süddeutsche Chemiefasern plant was announced in 1969 and the Phrix company, heavily dependent on staple fibre, closed down in 1971. The Glanzstoff company announced in the spring of 1971 their intention to shut down the largest German plant at Kassel.

Why can the EFTA producers, all of whom are small scale, except in Austria, continue to operate when large, technically efficient plants elsewhere are closing down? It is evident that in Norway, Sweden, Finland and Austria social considerations weigh more heavily in government policies than commercial factors. It is ironic that the Monopolies Commission's recommendation to terminate agreements with EFTA producers should have been carried out at a time when (as Courtaulds said in evidence) profits were about to decline anyway. This enabled state-influenced competitors, not animated by normal commercial considerations, to increase their share of the UK market.

The effect on Courtaulds of this change was not disastrous. It did not lead to any change in policy, other than the need to respond to the new price levels. Cash flow was reduced somewhat, but not to such an extent that required a rethinking of group policies. If, however, the inquiry and the subsequent government action had been a few years earlier, or if the whole procedure had been more speedy, it might have been more effective in diminishing group profits and in reducing the group's ability to carry through its other programmes. Delay was to the advantage of Courtaulds.

The recommendation about internal pricing was implemented, subject to the exception 'on purely commercial grounds.' Indeed, immediately following the hearing at which it became clear that there was a complete failure of understanding and therefore no prospect of understandable rules, it was decided to do away with any inhibitions which had existed and to be guided solely by the need for competitive, flexible pricing between divisions. This could—and occasionally did—lead to charging internal users more than the market price. For instance, in the depressed conditions of 1970 and 1971, when it was judged important to give the Group's stocking company managers every reason to hesitate about meeting some of the extremely low selling prices charged by their competitors, based on yarn supplied by Courtaulds' fibre competitors at special prices, they were required to use the Group's own nylon.

VERTICALISATION

The Monopolies Commission's 25 per cent market share recommendation about further acquisitions was not based on the same voluminous evidence as that supplied in connection with the cellulosic fibres covered by the terms of reference. Nevertheless, it influenced Whitehall attitudes for a while and caused some delay in the handling of some subsequent acquisitions. The Dell Committee was more important, but Courtaulds judged at the time that the encouragement it was given to go ahead with a polyester project was worth more than any loss suffered through not going ahead with the bid for English Calico; and nothing has happened since to modify that view.

The Lever Committee was more important for ICI than for Courtaulds, once it became clear that no attempt would be made to split Courtaulds' fibre from its textile activities. To have ICI as a strong vertical fibre-textile group would suit Courtaulds' interests taking a long view, because the interests of the two groups in dealing with Whitehall would coincide more than they would diverge, and it would thus strengthen any efforts to influence government policy.

COURTAULDS' IMAGE

It is an advantage for a large company to be well regarded. There are well-known examples of companies which have successfully created amongst the public generally an image of their corporate behaviour, necessarily over-simplified, in consequence of which the mention of those companies' names immediately produces an approving emotional response. The advantages extend into the firm's dealings with a number of sections of society—journalists and educators especially.

Courtaulds does not appear to have any clearly defined image in the sense described. Indeed, the speed with which the company and its range of activities have changed, and so recently, would make the existence of any such image unlikely; and the management have made no conscious effort in this direction. Much of what Courtaulds has done in the industry itself has clashed with the interests of those affected, and those who have suffered from the conflicts cannot be expected to speak warmly of the company. The fragmentation of the industry into so many firms, and the inevitable disappearance from business of many of them, has multiplied the number of such people.

There was a danger therefore that the extraordinary degree of attention which the company had received might affect adversely its public image, with consequences which it would be difficult to identify precisely; the Monopolies Commission report was a particular danger from this point of view.

ATTITUDES TOWARDS GOVERNMENT

The emotional response in Courtaulds to the failures of understanding which appeared in the inquiries, particularly with the Monopolies Commission, was to regard the whole Whitehall machine as beyond hope of influencing and incapable of understanding the management of businesses, and there was for a while a marked unwillingness to have any more contact than was absolutely necessary. In this respect there was a marked contrast with the earlier relationship concerning Lancashire. The change of government in June 1970, with an early inclination towards less intervention, provided a further reason for getting on with running the business without too much regard for the government machine.

The sheer weight of effort and diversion of time which the enquiries had caused were further and substantive reasons for wanting to get back to what was seen as a more normal, less involved relationship.

It is possible that if less resources had been expended by Courtaulds on these inquisitorial activities and if their outcome had not left such a feeling of bitterness and frustration, more initiative might have been devoted to formulating and pressing the case for a more coherent all-embracing international trade policy for textiles. Whether such an effort would have succeeded against the entrenched attitudes in support of opposing policies may be doubted, and as has been indicated a lot was attempted anyway. Despite periods of difficulty in the company's relations with Whitehall, Courtaulds' executives continued to participate actively but selectively in the deliberations of those Trade Associations which were regarded as responsible and effective channels for negotiation with government. But when it is seen what little progress has been made—except on a narrow front—and how important it is to achieve a fresh approach, the suspicion must arise that time and effort could have been more usefully deployed, and if there had not been also a subsequent turning away from Whitehall, much more could have been achieved.

Chapter Nine

THE PUBLIC INTEREST

Previous chapters have sought to examine the development of one business, government actions which affected it, and the interactions between them over a ten-year period, roughly 1960–70. They have described how it all appeared to those affected by government, as a contribution to the dialogue which is necessary to improve performance.

This final chapter will consider whether it is possible clearly to define the objectives of Courtaulds' management and of government in their respective fields, and if so whether and where these were compatible; and it will consider if there were clear criteria of performance by which to judge whether objectives were being achieved, and the extent to which the methods adopted gave rise to problems. Some general reflections are provoked by this attempt to bring into perspective the two sides of the government–industry interaction process in one particular case.

That the public interest requires a prosperous, expanding manufacturing industry is a commonplace of pronouncements from representatives of all three political parties. Public recognition is given to this belief, for example in the honours system and the Queen's Awards for technological achievement and export performance. Some might argue that this is an outdated attitude and that service industries with their contribution to invisible exports will in future be sufficient by themselves to support a rising standard of living for the UK; but welcome though the increased earnings are, they depend for their competitive pricing upon the continuing base-load of business which the needs of manufacturing industry provide, and this applies to all the service industries—banking, shipping, insurance, travel, and so on. So manufacturing industry remains the mainstay of the nation's economic activities.

But this carries no presumption about which manufacturing industries will (or should) survive and prosper and which will decline. That will be determined by changes in consumer demand, developments in technology, and the competitiveness of suppliers from overseas. In practice parts of any industry can be highly innovative and expansive, while other parts of the same industry may be in decline. Textiles are no exception.

It is the basis of the capitalist system that in general business decisions, made to suit the private interests of the individuals and enterprises concerned, will promote the social interest. Firms survive and make profits generally by making things which the public will buy at costs which reflect the value in alternative uses of the resources which are employed. Earning adequate profits to sustain business in fields in which the UK has a comparative advantage is in the social interest, as is investing in new technology which will ultimately benefit consumers. This is the chief reason why governments in this country usually have policies towards industry which see the primary role of government as 'holding the ring.'

But there can be no presumption that the private enterprise system can operate without government intervention to achieve the most desirable result. The imperfections of the system are too many and by now well identified. There are many situations in which government action is needed.

OBJECTIVES OF MANAGEMENT

The objectives of Courtaulds' management were reasonably clear. They had an interest in the survival of the company as an independent business, or if this proved impossible they would want to negotiate merger terms which would reflect credit on their ability as professional managers. Good profits and a general and well-founded belief in their continued increase were seen as essential to survival.

The commercial and investment strategy which was believed

to offer the best hope of achieving the objective emerged from a lengthy process, not always made explicit, of eliminating the alternatives.

The generally upward trend in profits which was seen as the objective took into account a three- to five-year period, the time-scale which seemed relevant to the investment and commercial factors with which management had to deal. Immediate profits had to take second place to doing what seemed necessary where an investment decision might take one to two years to translate into a usable plant, and where it might take two years or so to establish a viable commercial position with a new product or in an unfamiliar market.

It is often necessary for long-run efficiency to undertake expenditures which, looking at the firm as a whole, will appear to reduce profits and thus indicate reduced efficiency. For example, increasing market share at the expense of firms thought to be less efficient means investing cash in increased capacity, working capital and operating losses in order to achieve a better cost compared to competitors. Superior profit margin is rarely achieved without superior market share. Cash for this purpose must be derived from internal cash flow from all products and from external financing. There must be some profitable products for this to be possible and some belief that they will continue so.

The emphasis on a three- to five-year planning period was qualified by the need to take a much longer view for some purposes—research and management training and development, for example—and a much shorter view when considering investors' reactions to performance. The latter can often appear to be over-influenced by short-term considerations; yet they cannot be ignored for through their effect on the share price they affect the terms on which funds can be raised or acquisitions made, as well as the plans of possible takeover bidders. Management is thus preoccupied with rising profits both as the test of success and as the guarantee of their survival. The specific investment and commercial policy decisions which provide the interface between government and the company are subordinate to these overriding exigencies within the private enterprise system as it now operates.

G

OBJECTIVES OF GOVERNMENT

The experiences described in earlier chapters offer only limited perspectives, but even so the objectives of government are less easy to define than those of management.

A preliminary issue is whether these are essentially a response to pressures and thus capable of analysis only in political terms, or whether they reflect a rational economic and social assessment of the public interest. Bernard Crick in his *Defence of Politics* describes and justifies the political process in terms of the necessary balancing and reconciliation of conflicting interests. Certainly at times the interactions between Courtaulds and government seemed to be no more than incidental to such political imperatives as the marginal constituencies of Lancashire, or the need to be seen to be doing something about high unemployment in some localities.

These pressures can sometimes appear as the 'democratic imperative', an insistent and widespread public demand for action, such as that which led to the abolition of slavery (at which time, as the Royal Commission on Pollution pointed out in their First Report, a rational cost-benefit analysis might well have shown that slavery should have been preserved).

The relationship between a rational approach and the workings of the 'democratic imperative' is indeed tenuous. The Trade and Industry Sub-Committee of the Expenditure Committee of the House of Commons in its report (Session 1971–72) on 'Public Money in the Private Sector' recognises 'that the criteria will differ from Government to Government and that even within the lifetime of a single Government the emphasis may change considerably.' The list of the kinds of situation which could justify government financial intervention, where 'the free operations of the money market does not always meet national needs,' and include the need to maintain international competitiveness; defence requirements; the balance of payments; the maintenance of an industry considered nationally essential; the special difficulties of advanced-technology industries or projects; and social needs, especially the need to maintain employment.

The Sub-Committee were unable to extract from government witnesses 'any clear philosophy of criteria.' The question whether the country really needs a particular industry such as shipbuilding or aircraft manufacture found no firm answer; and the Sub-Committee's examination of individual situations in which aid has been given in recent years testifies to the variety of arguments which prevail and the absence of any coherent doctrine.

There is in this field no overwhelming consensus of public opinion, as there is for example on old-age pensions, as a result of which government actions can be regarded as a response to the 'democratic imperative.' A further difficulty is that governments have ideas and these are modified in the light of experience. The Sub-Committee found more emphasis at the end on the need to maintain employment.

However, the relationships between industry and government are much more than the by-product of political responses to pressures. There are too many continuing policies for that, even if the details of their execution may change from time to time. These include policies concerning international trade and tariffs, full employment, competition and a continuing preoccupation with growth (policy would be too strong a word, implying a belief in an ability to perform); and their existence implies rational objectives, capable of being expressed in economic and industrial terms.

Government action is thus a blend of responses to political pressures and attempts at economic rationality. Improved performance needs a wide consensus which will diminish the need for and the acceptability of those responses which are irrational when viewed in economic and social terms. The costs of achieving and maintaining a consensus can be high.

For government and for industry the administrative costs of interaction are considerable, and it is impossible to calculate the effects on industrial performance of diverting managers from their primary task of organising the efficient use of resources. The situations need to be clearly identified in which managements pursuing their private interests may affect the public interest adversely. The rules and procedures for dealing with possible conflict situations need to be as precise as possible, to save time and to avoid feelings of injustice. The contrast between the PIB and the Monopolies Commission is only in part one of personalities; it must also be ascribed in part to the clearer guidelines under which the PIB was acting.

This study has been concerned with a firm and an industry in which nationalisation is not an issue and public purchases are of relatively small importance. From this viewpoint the objectives of government have appeared to be:

1 Generally to let companies develop in whatever ways they can, within the framework imposed by company law, the financial and investment institutions, taxation and laws relating to specific aspects of industrial activity such as pollution.
2 But selectively to influence this process through negotiations about tariffs and other trade barriers. The general objective has been to work towards a freer world trade system but this has involved judgements, inherently difficult, about the impact on particular industries of the removal or imposition of barriers.
3 Government has sought further to influence the process of industrial development through regional policies designed to reduce disparities in employment.
4 General policies to encourage growth have taken the form, apart from exhortation, of incentives to invest.
5 Wages and prices have been brought under some form of control at intervals in attempts to check inflation.
6 A general belief in the need to foster competition has found expression in laws relating to restrictive practices and to monopolies and mergers and the institutions established to administer the legislation.

With a variety of objectives there is an inevitable variety of criteria. These are sometimes difficult to define. In consequence irrelevant criteria can be chosen or a wide discretion given to those who are responsible for advising on where the public interest lies. The events described in this study are chiefly interesting in looking at two areas in which these problems arise. First, government has to make its assessment of which industries should be helped to survive, where the doctrine of comparative advantage appears to be relevant. Second, government has to deal with possible divergences between public and private interest. These two aspects of policy require further discussion.

COMPARATIVE ADVANTAGE

Although there is a general acceptance that there is a long-term future for manufacturing industry in the UK, as was said earlier this does not involve the necessity that any specific industry should survive. The public interest requires that resources should be mobile between sectors and that GNP should be increased by shifting resources from sectors with relatively low productivity into those with relatively high productivity. This applies as much to individual enterprises as to whole sectors of an industry.

The doctrine of comparative advantage is no more than a logical demonstration that economic welfare can be improved for one country if it specialises in those activities in which it has a comparative advantage when compared with others. A country may be less efficient than others in all sectors of industry and yet improve welfare through international trade. This is why the UK can trade beneficially with the USA even though output per head is higher there than in the UK for practically every industry.

But relative costs change over the years as between one country and another. In part this may be associated with product life cycles. A mature technology in an industry becomes widely known internationally. In the early stages of a product's life cycle the crucial inputs are scientific and technological understanding, high risk finance and entre-preneurship. At later stages the crucial inputs may be low labour costs, a factory system that can tolerate mass produc-tion methods of working, and so on. At different phases of a product's life cycle, therefore, one country may have a greater or less comparative advantage in relation to other countries and consequently over time the international structure of production and trade will tend to change.

Those who had no confidence in any future for the Lanca-shire textile industry included some who believed that the comparative advantage in the production of Lancashire-type textiles had shifted to the less developed countries. As they saw it, government policy should encourage resources to move into other industries where they would contribute far more in terms of exports or import-saving than would be needed to replace the Lancashire-produced textiles.

Courtaulds believed that a proper consideration of comparative advantage did not inevitably lead to this conclusion. The decline could be reversed with enterprise, drive, investment in modern equipment and an appropriate economic environment provided by the government. Comparative advantage is a dynamic concept and can change significantly where rapid technological change is feasible. It is necessary, however, to look at potential future costs, taking into account the production levels which should be achievable. Where the decline of an industry has led to excessive high-cost capacity and a high level of imports, the government may have a role in providing transitional support, including measures to limit imports. In an industry which has been declining there may thus be a case for adopting the measures of protection which traditionally have been associated only with infant industries. A rebirth is as important as a new birth.

It is fundamental to the proposition that exchange rates are appropriate and reflect the average balance of efficiency between the trading nations. Inappropriate exchange rates will give the wrong indications as to the industries which should be expanding or declining. The signalling system is misleading. If sterling is persistently overvalued all industries are put under pressure, but most of all those which are struggling to survive.

Thus both in relation to exchange rates and to measures of protection the government has a key role in influencing the growth or decline of particular industries.

WHICH PUBLIC?

In looking at the public interest the UK is the relevant area. This does not mean that the interests of others—such as the lesser developed or the EEC—are ignored; they are a factor in any negotiations in which the UK is engaged, but only to the

extent that awareness of them, and of the possible consequences of flouting them, will influence the bargaining stance
which UK negotiators adopt.

This self-interested awareness of the interests of others is
illustrated in the conventions which have regulated international whaling for so many years. The increase in pollution
of various kinds may well make it desirable to negotiate other
conventions of much the same kind.

There are three reasons for adopting a strictly nationalistic
attitude. First this is the way in which the negotiators of other
nations behave and there is nobody else who will look after us
if ours do not act similarly. Secondly, the UK government is
accountable to the UK electorate and there is little evidence
that, by and large, the inhabitants of the UK are willing to deny
themselves for the sake of others. Thirdly, it is difficult enough
to discover and operate criteria for behaviour with UK
interests in mind; to attempt to go beyond this would remove
all possibility of rational behaviour.

In any discussion of the public interest we need to be clear
about the extent of the community which is considered as
relevant. The occasional wave of public emotion such as
inspired the anti-slavery movement must be seen as a departure
from the dictates of self-interest, requiring widely based public
support and providing no general rule for policy—especially
for a country which can no longer imagine itself to have the
wealth and international position to afford such initiatives.

In describing international trading policies concerning
textiles during the period, some ambivalence—even incon-
sistency—has been apparent. The government have had to
adjust to some conflicting and changing beliefs. These have
related to four topics. First has been the belief that the UK, as
a country dependent on international trade, has a particular
interest in the reduction and eventual removal of barriers to
trade. Second has been the realisation, as a result of experience, that in moving towards this objective UK industry's
ability to compete can be prejudiced if the effective barriers
which protect it are removed more quickly than those which
it has to surmount. Third has been the belief that the UK
needed to offer export opportunities to the developing

countries—with textiles as an obvious field. Fourth has been the belief that parts at least of the UK textile industry could not be competitive in modern conditions.

The changing intensity with which these beliefs have been held, and the interactions between them, have made it particularly difficult in the period under review to define the objectives of government policy.

UK membership of EEC is introducing a new factor, in terms of the opportunities for promoting UK interests which it will offer and the institutions through which those interests will be looked after. But it does not affect the essential argument. It will be many years before there are political institutions which substantially diminish the role of the nation state sufficiently to require a radically new approach to the debate on government–industry relationships.

SOCIAL AND PRIVATE INTERESTS

The divergences between social and private interest are the concern of government, even if they cannot all result in useful government action.

A divergence is not necessarily a conflict. Government can encourage managers to go further in certain directions than they might otherwise go by manipulating the rules of the game to bring private interests closer into line with the public interest.

Setting standards or criteria (chemical effluent, weight restrictions on roads, smoke control and so on) or providing specific tax incentives or subsidies (investment grants, regional incentives, and so on) are such attempts to manipulate private decisions in the public interest.

It is sometimes suggested that firms should be guided also by general expressions of public policy without the need for specific incentives or for rules binding on all. But this is to ignore the difficulties described in Chapter 4 of managing an enterprise: the profit and loss account does provide a logic to which all can be expected (hopefully) to conform, and to the extent that they do not it provides the test for corrective action by management. If it is supplemented by other imprecise and conflicting objectives, good management will be jeopardised. There has to be some separation of function for a workable society, and precise rules can help—just as within a firm the profit-maximising objective of the subordinate units has to be subject to overriding directives where the unit's activities would 'sub-optimise' the results of the whole.

Indeed, Eli Goldston goes further and argues in a US context[1] that changes in national goals have made GNP obsolete as a measure of national welfare; and he is not alone in this view. Growth in GNP looks a materialistic aim when set against other objectives such as assimilating minority groups, improving education, achieving truth in advertising, cultural enrichment, and protection of the environment. From this he derives the suggestion that private firms should prepare their own social accounts, dealing for example with minority employment, industrial safety and the adequacy of fringe benefits. Indeed, as President of a large corporation, he now provides shareholders with social as well as the usual financial accounts. Management is conceived as making choices between socially responsible conduct and net profit.

But the achievement of such objectives—however desirable —requires some use of scarce resources, and for a firm to pursue them is again to weaken the discipline of the profit and loss account and to provide confusing criteria of performance. If we all try to look after everything we shall get into a great muddle.

Perhaps we may follow the example of government in relation to the boards of nationalised industries. It appears now to be accepted (although the reality is rather different) that boards should concentrate on achieving their primary financial objectives, imposed with the authority of the law. If they are required to depart from the behaviour this would require, the Minister is expected to give a clear, written directive. There seems no reason to behave differently in dealings between government and private industry.

It follows from this that all business decisions which would involve departures from the private interests of the enterprises

[1] Eli Goldston, *The Quantification of Concern: Some Aspects of Social Accounting* (Carnegie-Mellon University, 1971).

concerned must be the subject of specific interventions or encouragements, administered in accordance with rules which are as precise as possible. And inability to frame precise rules must be a quite powerful argument for abstaining from intervention.

Any programme for improved arrangements in this field must concern itself with understanding criteria and procedure.

Yet even where there is much agreement on the objectives of policy, and where criteria can be set, great problems can arise. There is a general belief, for example, that industrial investment should be increased—in the public interest, yet successive governments have implemented quite different methods of trying to achieve this.

It may be that one system consistently applied over a long period might have been better. Industrialists would understand and take it as a certain factor in their calculations, and the administrators would improve their performances as a result of experience. This was happening with the arrangements for providing investment incentives through tax allowances. The system was understood by those who invest heavily and by the Inland Revenue officials who had operated the system for years. Disputes and misunderstandings seldom arose. The subsequent changes, however, have given rise to many problems. The time of the most active public debate may well have been the moment to leave the system alone.

However, as the Courtaulds experience shows, the result of all that was done probably was a substantially higher investment than would otherwise have been made.

The regional employment incentives were concerned with a much more easily identifiable test—the number of additional jobs which could be created in a particular region; the administrator's task was thus easier and the result testified to the success which was achieved.

But this does not necessarily mean that the right criteria were adopted. There is a limit to the expenditure which can be justified to maintain employment in a particular locality, as for example in dealing with the Upper Clyde shipworkers. To decide the expenditure which could be justified in the general interest would require an assessment of the cost of the alternatives, of which the most obvious would be to move and re-train for employment in areas of labour shortage—and the calculation must clearly include some measure of the intangible costs imposed on those who move from their familiar environment. It is of course likely that for some—old-age pensioners, for example—the costs of moving would be too high as compared with the costs to the community of their continued unemployment. There is obvious difficulty in making the assessment when industrial activity is generally at a low level, with no immediately apparent areas of labour shortage.

COMPETITION POLICY

The strand of government policy in relation to industry which has the longest history (apart from tariffs), and which is still extremely active—as this book has demonstrated—is competition and monopoly policy.

The monopolies legislation covers a field in which the criteria of the public interest are extraordinarily difficult to define. Individual case by case investigation, recommendation and decision are seen as the only solution.

Except perhaps in the United States, competition is not regarded as an end in itself; rather it is desired in order to achieve certain social objectives. It is through competition that certain benefits arise, and the nature of these expected benefits has helped to structure the legislation.

There is some consensus internationally on these broad objectives of competition policy, as can be ascertained from the Papers and Reports of the International Conference on Monopolies, Mergers and Restrictive Practices (organised by the Board of Trade in Cambridge in 1969). These may be summarised as follows:

1 An efficient use of resources within and between enter-prises, in the short run as well as in the long run.
2 A level of price no higher than necessary to provide an economic return to efficient enterprises.
3 A choice of goods or services for consumers, based upon

a recognition that there may exist many different segments of market demand.

4   Innovation, and the development of new processes, products, services and forms of organisation.

5   Fair trade between sellers and buyers, and fair competition between one seller (or potential seller) and
another.

Most emphasis in the literature generally is given to the safeguards against monopoly pricing, but this is perhaps one of
the least important aspects of competition policy. Studies of
this matter indicate that the costs of monopoly pricing to
consumers (the loss of consumer surplus) is very low, and
would not of itself justify the existence of an elaborate set of
rules and proceedings in this area of public policy. Much more
important are the effects of competition in the level of costs,
on the efficient allocation of resources, choice for consumers
and on innovation.

The foregoing paragraphs, reflecting the discussions at the
1969 Cambridge conference, show considerable realism, even
if criteria are difficult to establish. But in the absence of better
guides there has been a tendency to use as a criterion ideas
about competition which bear no relation to reality.

The intellectual model which appeared to have been
significant in the Commission's thinking in the cellulosic fibre
inquiry may have been influenced by the notions that perfect
competition produces an optimum allocation of resources,
and that situations of imperfect competition result in losses of
welfare. (Perfect competition is a technical concept, familiar
to economists.) Such a model based upon perfect competition
is coherent, a powerful tool of analysis, and no doubt of value
in the structure of economic theory.

But as a guide to policy about business, it is wrong and
wholly misleading. The fully extended model is static in
concept (for instance, research and development, and innovation have no part in it); it requires universality for its conclusions to follow; firms are usually not based on a single product
(so problems of overhead allocation arise); questions of
financing are ignored (or rather assumed away). While the

Commission never adhered to such an abstract and unrealistic formulation, they seemed to this author to have been influenced by it to an important degree.

Yet there is no adequate theory of the firm to take its place. As a guide to policy, J M Clarke's concept of 'workable competition' was an important advance. R Marris has made a valiant attempt to construct a more behavioural and managerial theory of the firm. What exists now is a rag bag of bits of theory that are most often difficult to test and always difficult to apply.

The absence of a single valid theory of the firm which has prescriptive value is not at all surprising, but it can lead those responsible for policy-making into considerable difficulty. The attempt to treat each case on its merits, admirable in principle, exposes the decision-maker to the inadequacies of these theories.

It has led many who have thought deeply about this problem to propose that the government should lay down clearly defined criteria of right and wrong business behaviour, for example about mergers, and should rely to a much smaller extent on judging the merits of each case.

What is needed most, however, is a better understanding of business behaviour and methods in government. Some of the concepts carried over from the earlier traditions of economics need to be reconsidered. For example, the concept of 'normal profit' is of doubtful validity. Business economists attempt to bridge this gap between the received economic doctrines of the theory of the firm, and the realities of business situations. It is fair to say that a wide gap remains. Yet the tools of economics, properly used, are useful in the analysis of business situations. That is not to be denied. Where the difficulties arise are in the concept of the public interest, for this evidently departs from the simpler notion of profit maximisation (or, more practically, profit improvement) which is so valuable as a control mechanism and as a guide to action in a firm.

Senior civil servants, pragmatists by reason of their role, will deny that their attitudes could reflect any such limited concept of the nature of competition. Even if this is so (and the 1969 White Paper—which must have been drafted by civil servants—refers to parts of the economy 'where conditions of even near perfect competition do not exist' as if that were a relevant concept), it is not necessarily true of those who accept part-time appointments on the bodies set up to administer legislation in this field. For example it is still possible for the PIB Fourth General Report (para 52) to provoke the comment: 'The influence of textbook teaching about so-called perfect competition lies heavily upon it.' (Professor T Wilson at the BOT conference on mergers, etc, in Cambridge in 1969.)

In 1960 Alan Neale wrote about the assumptions required for the 'perfect competition' model and the divergence between them and real world conditions. He suggested that the vocabulary of the subject had influenced thought; 'perfect' and 'pure' competition on the one hand and market 'imperfections' on the other can have psychological consequences. He concluded that competition may not be the appropriate concept for analysing the conditions of economic efficiency. The fundamental concept, he suggests, is mobility—the flow of resources to employments of maximum utility. Competition may be one means to mobility, but mobility can be achieved without competition, and in a contracting industry the process of adjustment may be retarded if left to competition alone. Oligopoly can be better for mobility than competition between a large number of firms.

The conflict between public and private interest is not so great as is believed by those who have in their minds an inappropriate concept of how competition operates. Markets are too narrowly defined. Apparent market power is subject to the threat of competitive plants being built by those who are attracted by the high profits which are believed to be made. There is always the threat of a takeover, however large the size of the company. Reverse takeover bids have often been successful. And entry into Europe shifts the whole discussion on to a different plane.

If government pursues policies where the criteria are difficult to define and where there is no consensus, even about which criteria are relevant, it is impossible to know what methods to adopt. So any success in achieving the broad purposes of government must be accidental. Management time is wasted. There is a sense of injustice and resentment. The useful interactions between industry and government are thus impaired.

Some may find comfort in the threefold process—first, the decision to refer, then the inquiry and its recommendations, and finally the decision on those recommendations. This, it is suggested, provides ample scope for a variety of representations and reflections on them to be taken into account before anything is done; and the limited eventual impact of the whole process on Courtaulds provides some support for this view. But the diversion of time and effort for so little useful result is difficult to justify.

If analysis is difficult it becomes impossible to devise sensible rules. Thus the preoccupation with textile industry structure described in earlier chapters was based upon notions about the share of markets which individual firms should be allowed to have. But to analyse such ideas in individual cases would require judgements about markets, potential costs and profits and the appropriate competitive behaviour. In some situations the public interest would lie in one firm supplying the whole market. The judgements are difficult enough for the firms directly concerned. To formulate rules which can be justified publicly would require more detailed attention than was given. So the rulings were effectively an acquiescence in what had happened, but with sufficient flavour of disapprobation to act as a check on further action by the firms concerned. Thus the preoccupation with structure had no useful results because, given the limited analysis which was possible in the circumstances, it could result in no clear rules of behaviour.

Whether rules binding on all need to have legislative form is an open question. The City Takeover Panel is a good example of a rule-making body, set up perhaps to forestall legislation, but possibly with advantages in being able to modify and develop its rules more flexibly than legislative procedures would permit. Improved arrangements for dealing with inadequate managements might also (conceivably) be achieved through some similar self-policing machinery.

UNDERSTANDING

Improved understanding on both sides should help. It might affect the choice of which interventions are felt to be useful, to shape more suitably those which cannot be avoided and to foster smoother working relationships in carrying them through. As will be apparent from the description of management methods in Chapter 4, there is little to be achieved through temporary secondment of civil servants into industry. It takes so long to acquire skill in getting things done within the special environment of any organisation, that the outsider is bound always to find himself in peripheral activities however useful. No doubt with few exceptions the same could be said of the temporary secondment of businessmen into the Civil Service. The permanent transfer of senior civil servants into executive management in industry has occurred from time to time, but the successes have been few in number. It is difficult to conceive of permanent transfers in the other direction on any scale which is likely to influence attitudes and methods of working.

So a more deliberate effort at improved understanding must accept the limited possibilities of transfers from one side to the other. The effort must therefore concentrate on those who are in full-time active employment in their respective spheres. The Civil Service have introduced into their internal training courses a substantial concern with government–industry relationships. There is nothing on a corresponding scale from the industrial side, though the leading business schools seek to improve understanding for the favoured few who attend their courses. The issues which matter are of course dealt with in industry only at a senior level. The management methods of industry require a less deliberate hierarchical distribution of information or consultation than those required to perform the completely different role of the Civil Service.

An important contribution to understanding can be derived from the employment as non-executive directors or consultants of those who have had senior experience—whether political or administrative—in government. Much help can be given by those with this experience, and there may be more scope for such appointments.

METHODS

In the account in Chapter 4 of the management methods which prevailed within Courtaulds during the period, there are doubtless a number of characteristics which are strikingly different from the methods which are appropriate to the handling of government business. The writer is conscious of some of these—the limited number of individuals involved in taking key decisions, the comparative absence of documentation, the speed with which decisions have to be taken and the consequent emphasis on making the decisions which have been taken come right, the comparatively short time-scale for which plans are made and results assessed, the absence of arrangements for public questioning of what is done provided that the overall results are acceptable; and there may well be others. Together they represent a pattern of behaviour which must be as unfamiliar to those in government as are the ways of government to those in industry.

Those concerned in the events described here drew a distinction between politicians and 'Whitehall,' but otherwise tended to regard civil servants and the agencies set up to administer the law as part of one single administrative machine. Workloads imposed from outside give rise to attitudes which do not discriminate too finely between the taskmasters. This emotional response to interventions goes along with a clear perception of respective powers and sanctions and a search (not always successful) for the right ways of handling each situation.

Corresponding to the variety of government objectives is a similar variety of departments and agencies each with its own staff with their own careers to look after. Unitary government is a myth. But unitary management was vital in the business situation described here, and their task was complicated by the variety of people—all, as they saw it, part of the Whitehall machine—with whom they had to deal, evidently with no one person aware of or appreciating the significance of what was being done.

So the dialogue needs to be at a senior management level. It might be possible for the larger firms at intervals to prepare a statement of their objectives in terms which are relevant to public policy, relating perhaps to investment plans, market targets, acquisitions, innovation and manpower plans. The extent to which government help and support would be needed and of what kinds could be discussed. The outcome would be a form of charter. Both sides would have to accept the inevitability of departures from it—political pressures from one side, new commercial pressures and opportunities from the other. With 400 firms accounting for some 80 per cent of UK manufacturing industry, the task should not be too formidable. The existence of such charters should speed up and simplify the handling of other interactions.

The government would naturally need to remain free to intervene under the law wherever a firm might be acting in ways contrary to the public interest. The charter and its related discussions would then be useful evidence.

The Textile Council study was, in a crude form, one step in preparing such a charter.

IMPROVED CRITERIA

The interest of the public as a whole is a concept which is not easily identified through the normal political and administrative processes. Sometimes it is particularly difficult to find the criteria.

The Commission on the Third London Airport was one attempt to deal with this issue. The Commission sought to balance the conflicting considerations on where the airport should be located by an assessment of costs and benefits (the intangible as well as the measurable) of alternative solutions in order to arrive at a rational decision. The public interest was identified with the outcome of a rational process taking into account all those interests affected by the decision as to timing and location.

The Commission's recommendation was not influenced by

political considerations and in the event was rejected by the then government (Conservative). It can be argued that the Commission should have tempered its findings by reference to what might have been politically acceptable, but this surely misrepresents the function of a body of this kind. To present for public discussion an assessment which is based upon some rational criteria of the public interest must be a part of society's arrangements for taking decisions, even if other, less rational, considerations sometimes prevail in the end.

To provide guidelines for industry which are disclosed to all who need guidance will require some organising. In dealing with competition policy the Monopolies Commission might well be the means for doing the work if it had a suitable research team and were to hold public hearings. Then, following the pattern of the Roskill Commission, the research team's findings on these contentious issues could be made available for debate without the Commission being committed. Public hearings could then give the Commission the basis for a report which might reflect some consensus and thus be the more capable of application. The Minister's role would be to accept or reject these findings.

This would steer a middle course between erratic judgements of where the public interest lies which arises in the absence of clear definitions and the disadvantages of the more rigid US rules of behaviour. The process should result in a document unlike the Board of Trade 'Handbook on Mergers,' which lists everything with no systematic way of analysing the various factors.

The argument of this study has been that monopoly pricing (according to the textbook) for certain products and periods can be a necessary feature of the arrangements for securing the benefits of a more realistic competition policy; and this accords with industrial experience which shows that no important moves are made without the prospect of a sustained period of good profits. If policy really were aimed at achieving the text-book result, and were successful, little innovation of any kind would occur.

A business is a portfolio of risk situations. Products—even successful products—have life cycles; some are unexpectedly short, others extend over longer periods. Turning points are difficult to predict because of technological change and market developments. Any investigation is likely to find some products at the peak of their earning capacity, and others on their way up or on their way down. Therefore a snapshot at one point of time of this set of risk situations will be meaningless in terms of understanding the dynamics of a business, and criticisms of high earnings at the peak may well be wholly misplaced. Without the prospect of peak cash earnings, the urge to grow and to embark upon new risk situations would be inhibited; and the feasibility of embarking upon new risk situations would be reduced if earnings were cut off at their peak for the sake of so-called monopoly considerations.

If realism dictates that the monopoly profit test is abandoned, those concerned with public policy must form judgements about the quality of management's use of resources well before trading results are available to show whether good or bad decisions have been made.

It will be necessary to search for acceptable ways of measuring efficiency. Efficiency can only be assessed by reference to the best practice in other situations. This criterion is not good enough for management; they should be seeking to outdo their competitors. But for public interest purposes the 'best practice' test is the only practicable one. Any performance in the company being investigated which is better than that is a bonus. But the 'best practice' test requires international comparisons—of prices, costs, the speed with which innovations are introduced and so on. A concern with firms rather than with products will play a more important part in the assessment than was apparent in the case studied here.

The assessment of potential added value might well be a key measurement—potential rather than past or present for obvious reasons, though this means abandoning the apparent certainty of statistics; and the assessment for an individual firm must take account of those relating to firms in the preceding and subsequent stages of manufacture; to the extent that their continued existence is essential to realising the potential foreseen by the individual firm. Thus in the case studied here the past low net added value per head of employment in the UK garment industry (by comparison with the average for all industry) and the prospects for improving it must be a factor in considering the comparatively high figures for manmade fibres and the rising figures for fibre–fabric conversion.

The qualification to this lies in the extent to which the apparent added value figure is distorted by monopolistic behaviour (properly defined) or by inefficiencies. So added value is not a simple test. However, if properly used it can be an indicator which links the assessment of the public interest with criteria which are also relevant to good management.

INSTITUTIONS

The job of identifying divergences of interest and formulating policies and rules for removing them is essentially for government. The institutional arrangements will need to provide for a proper understanding in government of the likely effects of proposed policies and rules. Given the limited scope for interchange of people, this understanding must come in part through the established procedure of setting up bodies with experienced people from both sides to examine and report on specific issues.

The latter presents problems where selective interventions are at issue. The experienced people whose views are most worth having are those with an axe to grind. The conflicting arguments about para-governmental agencies in this field are rehearsed in the Sub-Committee's report (Chapter 7) and follow predictable lines. Businessmen, it is argued, are more able than civil servants to deal with the kind of issues which arise, there is advantage in independence from government, whilst retaining the ultimate sanction of government authority. The case against such an agency rests on the greater scope for *ad hoc* treatment within a government department, the accumulated experience of civil servants in monitoring public money in the private sector, the working of the private capital system might be impaired, parliamentary control would be weakened. More interesting, however, is the argument in Chapter 8 that whereas government might be inclined to take a decision on unquantified social grounds, an agency would be under greater discipline to put figures to admittedly imprecise notions of social costs and benefits. Thus arises again the issue of the conflict between decisions resulting from political pressures and those reflecting some more rational assessment of the public interest.

The Sub-Committee was concerned only with direct financial aid to private industry, but other kinds of relationship with government which are specific to a firm or an industry also require a disciplined attempt to assess costs and benefits before precise rules can be devised. This is the useful area for para-government agencies. Their attempts at rational assessments may not always prevail against political pressures, but increased understanding and rationality might be expected in time to have some influence.

The writer's experience as a member of the Commission on the Third London Airport was a useful opportunity to examine the way in which earlier examinations of the problem had been conducted within the Civil Service; and provides some confirmation of the Sub-Committee's view that an external agency, attempting to quantify and submitting the evidence to public scrutiny, can force all concerned into devoting the time and skills which are needed in the attempt to achieve rational solutions—though the cost is high and this is a further reason for limiting the number of 'public interest' investigations.

The issues which might be suitable for consideration by para-government agencies would relate to the desirable scale of domestic industry in relation to the market, the extent to which private industry needs help in achieving the desirable, and the appropriate kinds of help; and to those possible divergences between public and private interest which government are persuaded to look into.

A typical ministerial statement will contrast the interests of the industry with the other factors which government has to take into account, such as the consumer, 'the UK's vital political and economic stake in the prosperity of developing countries' and the minister's function of striking 'the best balance in the national interest.' This study has been critical of some of the concepts and some of the institutional arrangements which have ruled in this field. A greater acceptance that the interests of industry and those of the public generally march in step, improved concepts, greater rationality and improved institutions might be expected in time beneficially to influence the way in which the balance is struck.

Appendix A

MAN-MADE FIBRES COMPARED WITH NATURAL FIBRES—ORIGIN, FORM, AND USES

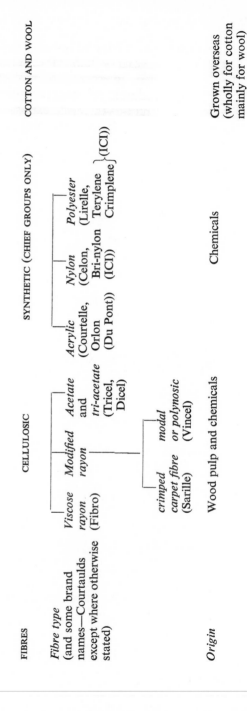

FIBRES	CELLULOSIC			SYNTHETIC (CHIEF GROUPS ONLY)			COTTON AND WOOL
Fibre type (and some brand names—Courtaulds except where otherwise stated)	*Viscose rayon* (Fibro)	*Modified rayon* — *crimped carpet fibre* (Sarille) / *modal or polynosic* (Vincel)	*Acetate and tri-acetate* (Tricel, Dicel)	*Acrylic* (Courtelle, Orlon (Du Pont))	*Nylon* (Celon, Bri-nylon (ICI))	*Polyester* (Lirelle, Terylene Crimplene) (ICI)	
Origin	Wood pulp and chemicals			Chemicals			Grown overseas (wholly for cotton mainly for wool)

Usual fibre form for further process	Staple, filament	Staple	Largely filament; tow	Staple, tow and tops	Filament (and some staple)	Staple, filament	Staple	Staple

FURTHER PROCESSES

Spinning—producing yarn by spinning together short fibre lengths obtained in the form of staple or tops.

Weaving—production of fabric from filament or spun yarn by combining weft threads (horizontal) with warp threads (vertical).

Knitting—(a) warp knitting—largely from filament yarn and typically for lingerie, furnishing, lining fabrics.
(b) weft knitting—from filament or spun yarn, mainly of outerwear fabrics (very often known as 'jersey' fabrics).

Making-up—producing articles of clothing or other finished articles by cutting and assembly of fabrics.

END USES

All fibres referred to here are used for textiles production: garments, household textiles and furnishings, either alone or in blends, e.g. polyester/cotton, wool/nylon, polyester/viscose.

Acetate tow is used for cigarette filter tip production.

Viscose, nylon and polyester high tenacity filament are for industrial uses, such as tyre cord and belting.

Notes

1 staple—short lengths of fibre for spinning into yarn.
2 filament—continuous fibre length; yarn composed of several filaments—multifilament yarn.
3 tow—continuous fibre lengths in a loose strand.
4 tops—short fibre lengths produced by stretch-breaking tow of synthetic fibre, or by carding and combing wool (or m.m.f. staple) for spinning into yarn.

Appendix B

COURTAULDS' SHARE IN MAJOR SECTORS OF UK TEXTILE PRODUCTION (at 1971 Values)

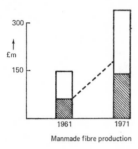

Manmade fibre production

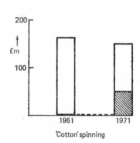

'Cotton' spinning

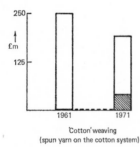

'Cotton' weaving
(spun yarn on the cotton system)

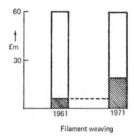

Filament weaving

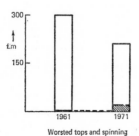

Worsted tops and spinning

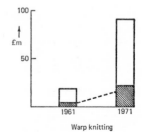

Warp knitting

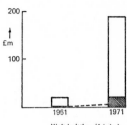

Weft knitting (fabrics)

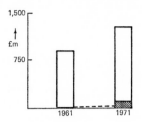

Garments and household textiles

KEY

 Industry production in sector indicated (£m)

 Courtaulds production in sector indicated (£m)

 This point on the 1971 bar indicates what Courtaulds production would have been in 1971 if it had had <u>the same share of the total industry production</u> by value as it achieved in 1961.

Thus in 1971 Courtaulds was producing about twice the value of manmade fibres as it did in 1961, but its actual <u>share</u> of total value of production in the U K in 1971 was less than it was in 1961.

Index